Gorbachev!
Has the Real
Antichrist Come?

Gorbachev! Has the Real Antichrist Come?
© Copyright 1988 by Robert W. Faid
ISBN 0-932081-19-3
All rights reserved.
Printed in the United States of America.

Published by Victory House, Inc.
P.O. Box 700238
Tulsa, Oklahoma 74170

Gorbachev!
Has the Real Antichrist Come?

By
Robert W. Faid

VICTORY HOUSE PUBLISHERS
Tulsa, Oklahoma

This book is dedicated to
Polycarp, Ignatius, Germanicus, Justin
and all Christian martyrs,
known and unknown,
past, present — and future.

May God give us all that same measure
of faith and courage
to proclaim Jesus Christ as Lord
until the very end of time.

Preface

This will not be a pleasant book to read. For many it will be terrifying. Others will dismiss what it says entirely, calling it foolishness. Some, I pray, will take warning and begin to get spiritually ready for what is to come.

I did not want to write this book. It actually began about 1:00 AM on March 8, 1985, when I was awakened with a tremendous sense that something of great importance was about to happen. I was led by the Lord into the Book of Revelation. The Lord showed me what the ten kingdoms and the ten horns of Revelation's prophecy might mean in relation to the Soviet Union and the Communist Bloc nations. Three days later Konstantin Chernenko died suddenly and Mikhail Sergeevich Gorbachev was elected by the Politburo as General Secretary of the Soviet Communist Party.

This book matches the antichrist prophecy with what we know of Gorbachev. It also looks at the current world situation in terms of the fulfillment of biblical end-times prophecy. It also forecasts what must happen in order for those prophecies to be fulfilled.

This book was completed over a year before its publication. In that time some events which it forecasted have already taken place. When possible the chapters have been updated to include these events which had already been forecasted as necessary for Gorbachev to accomplish his purpose.

I ask that you read this book with an open mind. Some things it contains may be contrary to what you believe or have heard. But please take what it says seriously. There is very little time left to prepare yourself to face what is certain to come.

Only with God's help can any of us face it.

Contents

Introduction — The Antichrist Prophecy

There has been intense interest and much speculation about the beast which John saw rising from the sea — the antichrist — ever since the apostle shared his vision of the end times in the book of the Revelation. Such interest is understandable because the appearance of this man (the antichrist) marks the final stages of the world as we know it.

Throughout history people have accused many men of being this "man of sin." It is probable that the first who was so accused was the Roman emperor Nero. He did indeed persecute thousands of Christians, killing untold numbers. But Nero was not the antichrist, for it was not time for him to make his appearance on the world scene. Several popes have been branded as the antichrist, and many Protestant leaders have been similarly accused by Catholics. Many thought Adolf Hitler might be the one, and Hitler was indeed an evil man. But none of these men could have been the true antichrist, for it was not time for him to appear. The time has now come, however, and the antichrist is in power today. The final countdown of the end times has begun.

Will the Real Antichrist Please Stand Up?

There is only one way to recognize him, and that is to study the prophecies concerning him in John's Revelation. This final book of the Bible contains all the clues we need.

Let us examine John's prophecy and contrast it with a man who is alive and in power today — a man who is in position to bring about the very events which John saw in his vision of the end times.

His name is Mikhail Sergeevich Gorbachev.

He is the General Secretary of the Soviet Communist Party.

He is the leader of the Soviet Union and the Soviet bloc nations.

He is commander-in-chief of the mightiest military force ever assembled.

He sits in the seat of power of an ideology that has world domination as its avowed aim.

The atheistic communist doctrine he represents is diametrically (and diabolically) opposed to the Judeo-Christian principles on which the Free World is based.

New Testament Antichrist Prophecy

The coming of the antichrist was foretold by the Apostle John in the Revelation and by other writers in the New Testament. Paul calls him "the son of perdition" and "the man of sin": "Let no man deceive you by any means: for that day shall not come, except there come a falling away first, and that man of sin be revealed, the son of perdition: Who opposeth and exalteth himself above all that is called God, or that is worshipped: so that he as God sitteth in the temple of God, showing himself that he is God" (2 Thess. 2:3, 4).

Paul is telling us that before the antichrist comes into the world there will be a great falling away of Christians from their faith. People's hearts will grow so cold toward God that they will be ready and willing to worship the antichrist as the solver of the world's problems.

Jesus told His disciples about what was to come in the end times and what to look for: "For false Christs and false prophets shall rise, and show signs and wonders, to seduce, if it were possible, even the elect. But take heed: behold, I have foretold you all things" (Mark 13:22, 23).

We will also examine just what Jesus told His disciples about what to expect and what the signs of the end times will be, when the antichrist and the false prophet will try to deceive the world, and replace the worship of God with the worship of Satan and his agent —the antichrist.

We Have All the Clues We Need to Identify Him

1. He will appear abruptly, like a sea monster rising from the sea.
2. He will have seven heads.
3. He will have ten horns and ten crowns.
4. He will rule ten countries in addition to his own.

5. Upon each head the name of blasphemy will be written.
6. He will be like a leopard.
7. His feet will be those of a bear.
8. His mouth will be that of a lion.
9. The dragon will give him his power, his seat, and great authority.
10. He will be the eighth king of a country.
11. Ten other kings will give their strength and power to him.
12. They will have no power of their own, but will serve at his discretion.
13. These ten kings will be of one mind (ideology) with the antichrist.
14. The number of his name will be connected with 666.
15. One of his heads will have a deadly wound.
16. This wound will be dramatically healed and the world will be astonished.

While examining these clues, we will also look at the world situation and compare it with end-times prophecy to determine whether the time is right for the antichrist to come upon the world scene.

We will also attempt to predict, using the Revelation prophecy and the shape of world events, just what the antichrist will do in order to conquer the world — as John's vision of the end times tells us he will do.

Please read these chapters with an open mind. They may contain some things which are quite contrary to what you have been taught or told to expect. But the Creator has given each of us a mind to use and a free will to exercise. Use them both — for your eternity may well depend on your decisions.

1

666 — The Number of His Name

But the very hairs of your head are all numbered. (Matt. 10:30)

Science without religion is lame, religion without science is blind. (Albert Einstein)

How does the number 666 relate to the name of Mikhail S. Gorbachev? The amazing numerical system represented by 666 is used in subsequent chapters of this book to reveal some startling clues to the end-times prophecy and the coming of the antichrist into the world.

"Let those who are able, interpret this code: the numerical values of the letters in his name add to 666" (Rev. 13:18 *TLB*).

In the time when John wrote this prophecy concerning the antichrist, there were no Arabic numerals. In order to write down a number, a person either had to spell it out, or — and this is what we are after — use certain letters which had known numerical values.

Many languages used a system that gave numerical values to the letters of the alphabet. Greek and Hebrew are two such languages, and everyone who used these languages knew exactly what number each letter represented. Exhibit I lists each Greek and Hebrew letter and the number each represents.

These were values employed during the time when the Old Testament was written in Hebrew and in John's time when the New Testament was written in Greek. We are going to decipher some hidden clues in biblical prophecy, using the values of these letters, and see for ourselves an amazing numerical system woven into the Scriptures, a system that defies human explanation.

EXHIBIT I Numerical Values of Hebrew and Greek Letters

HEBREW ALPHABET		GREEK ALPHABET	
א	1	α	1
ב	2	β	2
ג	3	γ	3
ד	4	δ	4
ה	5	ε	5
ו	6	ς'	6[2]
ז	7	ζ	7
ח	8	η	8
ט	9	θ	9
י	10	ι	10
כ-ך	20[1]	κ	20
ל	30	λ	30
מ	40[1]	μ	40
נ	50[1]	ν	50
ס	60	ξ	60
ע	70	ο	70
פ-ף	80[1]	π	80
צ-ץ	90[1]	ο	90[2]
ק	100	ρ	100
ר	200	σ-ς	200[1]
ש	300	τ	300
ת	400	υ	400
		φ	500
		χ	600
		ψ	700
		ω	800

(1) These letters are the same. The second letter is used when it occurs as the last letter in a word.

(2) These letters existed at the time of the writing of the New Testament but later became extinct.

The Secret Code Solved

A book was published in 1977 which revealed what the authors described as 'God's best-kept secret.' This book, *Theomatics* [1], has revealed an interlocking numerical system in the Scriptures which defies logical explanation. In fact, even with our state-of-the-art computers, it is impossible to duplicate this system in just one language. Nonetheless, it is contained in both the Hebrew of the Old Testament and the Greek of the New Testament. The only possible explanation is that God put this system there for *this generation to discover.*

The Theomatic Number System

Jerry Lucas and Del Washburn found that there are certain numbers, which they call theomatic numbers, that are capable of being divided into the total numerical values of words, phrases and even entire passages of the Scriptures with no remainder or within a cluster principle explained in their book. The number 666 is such a theomatic number.

To illustrate how this system works — and to find another theomatic number which we will use later in this chapter — let us count up the values of the individual letters in the Greek spelling of JESUS. This spelling has been taken from *The Interlinear Greek-English New Testament* [2].

John 4:1 Jesus
Ιησους

$$
\begin{array}{rcl}
\text{I} &=& 10 \\
\eta &=& 8 \\
\sigma &=& 200 \\
\text{o} &=& 70 \\
\upsilon &=& 400 \\
\varsigma &=& 200 \\
\hline
&& 888
\end{array}
$$

The total value of the Greek letters in the name of Jesus is 888.

Another way this may be expressed is 111 x 8, for when we divide 888 by 111 we get 8. The number 111 is a theomatic number and it is found throughout the Scriptures representing Jesus Christ.

This is illustrated by the following:

Christ	111 x 12
Χριστον"	
God	111 x 5
τον θεον'	
Lord	111 x 9
κυριου	
Lord Jesus	111 x 11
κυριε Ιησου"	
Christ the Lord	111 x 21
Χριστον κυριου'	
My beloved Son	111 x 14
υιον μου αγαπητον'	

You can see from these illustrations that whenever a word or phrase in the Scriptures refers to Jesus Christ, the value of the total individual letters is divisible by the theomatic number 111.

666 — The Theomatic Number of the Antichrist

The theomatic number of the antichrist is given to us in the Scriptures: "The one therefore having wisdom, let him calculate the number of the beast: for it is the number of man, and it is 666" (Rev. 13:18).

This was taken from the Chester Beatty Papyrus, the oldest-known manuscript of the book of Revelation. Let's look at the Greek text of this passage and add up the value of all of the individual letters in it.

εχων ουν ψηφισατω αριθμον του θηριου αριθμος γαρ ανθρωπου εστιν εστιν δε χξς

The total is 9990. When we divide this by 666 we get 15.
This may be expressed as 666 x 15.

Not only does this verse tell us that the antichrist will have a name which is a function of 666 but it is, itself, a function of the theomatic number 666. Let's look at another passage of the Scriptures where the antichrist is discussed: "Children, it is the last hour; and just as you heard that antichrist is coming..." (1 John 2:18).

παιδια εσχατη ωρα εστιν και καθως ηκουσατε οτι αντιχριστος ερχεται᾽

When we add up these Greek letters and divide by 666, we get:

666 x 12

Here is another verse: "The man of sin, the son of perdition..." (2 Thess. 2:3).

ανθρωπος ανομιας υιος της απωλειας᾽

When we add up the value of the Greek letters and divide by 666 we find it is equal to 666 x 6.

So we see that the number 666 is a theomatic number and that it is found in the Scriptures where the antichrist is spoken of. But our candidate, Mikhail S. Gorbachev, is Russian. In what language should we spell his name to look for the relationship with 666? Is Russian a theomatic language also?

The Cyrillic or Russian Alphabet

The Cyrillic alphabet was derived from Greek in the ninth century. Two Greek missionaries, Cyril and his brother Methodius, lived and worked among the Slavic people in what later came to be known as central Russia. They translated the Bible from the Greek into the Slavic tongue, but to do this they first had to develop a new alphabet to reflect the sounds peculiar to that language.

If the Cyrillic letters were derived from Greek, then perhaps the early Slavs used these letters in place of numbers. They did, indeed. Linguistic research tells us that four of the original Cyrillic symbols had no sound equivalent at all; their total function was to designate a number.

Figures Don't Lie

In the course of history many men have been accused of being the antichrist. Many people have played games with various alphabets in order to make the names of candidates come out to the required 666. By playing games with any alphabet, we could make *any* name come out to 666, or a multiple of it. To tell you the truth, if you would allow me to play games with the English alphabet, I could make even *your* name come out to 666. But I am sure you agree that this is not legitimate.

The individual who proposed that Henry Kissinger was the antichrist played games with the English alphabet. His contrived values made each succeeding letter worth six more than the last. For instance, *a* was equal to 6, *b* was 12, *c* was worth 18, etc. With this contrived value system, the name Kissinger does equal 666.

Let us then take the Russian alphabet, just as any child in the Soviet Union learns his "ABC's" and assign numerical values exactly as they are assigned to Greek and Hebrew. I consulted a Russian language book, *Hugo's Russian Grammar* [3], and used the same sequence of letters that is shown there. No games were played in assigning numerical values to the Cyrillic letters. This is shown in Exhibit II.

The exact spelling of Gorbachev's name in Russian was furnished to me by an old friend, Dr. P. Andrew McCormick, professor of Russian at Loyola College in Baltimore, Maryland. He also supplied the English transliteration of his name.

MIKHAIL SERGEEVICH GORBACHEV

МИХАИЛ СЕРГЕЕВИЧ ГОРБАЧЕВ

I doubt that one person in ten thousand in the western world has ever heard Gorbachev's middle name. He has been presented to us as either Mikhail S. Gorbachev or simply Mikhail Gorbachev. Using his full middle name did not yield anything meaningful, but when the middle initial was used, the following theomatic value was found:

Mikhail S. Gorbachev

МИХАИЛ С. ГОРБАЧЕВ''' = 666 X 2

Our candidate's name, when spelled in his native tongue, yields a number which is a function of 666.

EXHIBIT II The Russian Alphabet

Letter	Numerical Value	English Equivalent	Letter	Numerical Value	English Equivalent
Аа	1	A (ah)	Рр	80	R
Бσ	2	B	С	90	S
В	3	V	Т	100	T
Г	4	G	У	200	U (oo)
Д	5	D	Ф	300	F
Ее	6	E	Х	400	Like CH in loch
Ж	7	Like S in measure	Ц,	500	TS
З	8	Z	Ч	600	CH
И	9	I	Ш	700	SH
Й	10	I short	Щ,	800	SH-TCH
К	20	K	Ъ	900	Hard Sign
Л	30	L	Ы	1000	YEH-RE
М	40	M	Ь	2000	Soft Sign
Н	50	N	Є	3000	A (ay)
О	60	O	I-О	4000	U(yoo)
П	70	P	Я	5000	YAH

Gorbachev in Hebrew

Hebrew, as we have seen, is also a theomatic language. I consulted several Hebrew language experts to obtain an accurate transliteration of Gorbachev's name in Hebrew.

Two of the scholars I conferred with are Rabbi Hyman Fishman of

Beth Israel Synagogue in Greenville, South Carolina, and Dr. Terry Rude, professor of Hebrew at Bob Jones University. I found that modern Hebrew is a very imprecise language and that there were a number of equally correct transliterations of Gorbachev's name. One of these, in which the maximum number of Hebrew letters is used, was found to give an exact function of the number 666. Since so many variations exist, the theomatic function of this transliteration in Hebrew will not be used to calculate the mathematical probabilities of Gorbachev being the antichrist. This transliteration is given below:

Mikhail Sergeevich Gorbachev

מיכאל סצרגייזזיטש גארביטטששאזן equals 666 X 2

Gorbachev in Greek

I consulted also with Dr. Roy E. Lindahl, Professor of Classical Languages at Furman University. He transliterated our candidate's name in Greek for me. Using the standard known values for the Greek letters resulted in the following:

Mikhail S. Gorbachev

Μιχαηλ Σ. Γορμβαχοβ' equals 888 x 2, or 111 x 16

And: Gorbachev

Γορμβαχοβ equals exactly 888, or 111 x 8

What an astonishing coincidence! The name of our candidate in Greek has exactly the same theomatic value as the true Jesus Christ in Greek! His last name has *exactly* the same theomatic value as the name of Jesus has in Greek.

What more exact opposites could there be than the true Christ and the antichrist? But this is not surprising for we are about to see that sometimes direct opposites *do* have the same theomatic values.

The theomatic number 100 has been found to designate such subjects as light, truth and power. But it has also been found that 100 can designate direct opposites of these. Let's examine some examples:

Luke 11:35	Light	φως	equals 100 x 15
John 1:5	Darkness	δκοτια'	equals 100 x 6
Acts 9:18	Eyes	οφθαλμων	equals 100 x 15
Matthew 15:14	Blindness	τυφλος	equals 100 x 15
Matthew 6:22	Clear eye	οφθαλμος απλους'	equals 100 x 17
Matthew 6:23	Evil eye	οφθαλμος πονηρος"equals 100 x 15
Romans 11:8	Eyes to see	οφθαλμους βλεπειν"equals 100 x 15
Romans 11:8	See not	του μη βλεπειν	equals 100 x 10

From just these few examples we can see that opposites can sometimes have exactly the same theomatic numerical designations. The names Gorbachev and Jesus, which have diametrically opposite meanings, therefore have the same theomatic number designating them. I believe this is another sign God has placed before us to help us identify the true antichrist.

Satan's Theomatic Number

We would expect Satan to have his own theomatic number, and he does. This number is 276. Let's look at some Scriptures in Greek which have to do with Satan:

Satan	Σατανα'	equals 276 x 2
The evil one	τω πονηρω	equals 276 x 8
The dragon	τω δρακοντι'	equals 276 x 6

The prince of the power of the air	equals 276 x 15
τον αρχοντα της εξουσιας του αερ0ς"	

Beelzebub, the ruler	equals 276 x 6
Βεεζεβουλ αρχοντι'	

And to show that the same theomatic numbers hold true for the Old Testament as well as the New Testament and for Hebrew as well as

Greek, let's look at Isaiah 14:12: "How art thou fallen from heaven, O
Lucifer, son of the morning."

איך בפלת משמים הילל פן שחר   equals 276 x 6

Now let's compare some of the same words in Greek and Hebrew.

Genesis 2:9	Evil זרצ	equals 276
Matthew 5:39	Evil τω πονηρω	276 x 8
Genesis 6:12	All flesh כל בשר	276 x 2
Hebrews 12:9	The flesh τους μεν σαρκος	276 x 6

Satan and the Antichrist

I am sure that by now you understand what theomatic numbers are
all about. We have seen that the number 666 is connected with the
antichrist and that the number 276 designates Satan. Since the
antichrist will be Satan's agent on earth in the last days, shouldn't we
expect them to also be theomatically related? Let's look at the word
'antichrist.'

I John 2:22   antichrist   equals 666 x 2.76
         αντιχριστος'   or conversely, 276 x 6.66
And another reference to him:

Revelation 13:15 The image of the beast   equals 666 x 2.76
         τη εικονι του θηριου   or conversely, 276 x 6.66

The Hidden Clue —The Number of Man

Man also has a number and it is very interesting just how this
number is derived. In both Hebrew and Greek, the word for man and
the word for Adam, the first man, are identical. Let's write these out
and count up their numerical values:

Genesis 5:2	Adam (man)	אדמ'	equals 46
Romans 5:14	Adam (man)	Αδαμ	equals 46

Why should man's number be 46? Can we find any reason why it should be this particular number? Yes, and modern science helps us to find this answer. All living things are products of genetics and each species carries a unique configuration of the DNA molecules which determines not only the characteristics of that individual, but determines *just what type* of living organism will be produced. Each different species carries genes which differ from every other species in number, shape and configuration.

Genetically, man has forty-six chromosomes.

Forty-six is truly the *number of man*.

Man and Satan

For thousands of years certain numbers have been recognized as representing certain things. The number seven has stood for perfection, while the world is less than perfect and is represented by the number six, one less than perfection. To illustrate the world's number, let's look at the following:

John 1:10	World κοσμος	equals 600 or 6 x 100
Revelation 19:2	Earth γην'	equals 60 or 6 x 10

We have seen that man's number is 46. Now when man (46) lives according to the world (6), we get the following:

$$46 \times 6 = 276 \text{ — the number of Satan!}$$

The Hidden Clue to the Antichrist

Now still in connection with the number of man (46), we must go back and look at the wording of Revelation 13:18. Greek is a peculiar language in that there are no rules for articles. A sentence in Greek would read exactly the same whether or not the articles 'the,' 'a,' or 'an,' are included. We could, therefore, read the passage in Revelation 13:18 in the following ways:

"...for it is the number of *a* man..."
     or equally correct:
"...for it is the number of man...."

And what is the 'number of man'? It is 46.

Therefore, the name of the man who is the true antichrist should have a numerical value which is both a function of 666, *and the number of man which is 46.*

This leads us to examine the transliterations of Gorbachev's name again in Russian.

Mikhail S. Gorbachev
МИХАИЛ С. ГОРБАЧЕВ' equals 46 X 29

Mikhail Gorbachev
МИХАИЛ ГОРБАЧЕВ'''   equals 46 X 27

The Russian spelling of his name is a function of both 666 and 46. Now let's see what the Hebrew transliteration will give us.

Mikhail Sergeevich Gorbachev
מיכאל סצרגייןזיטש גארביטטששאןן equals 46 x 29

The Antichrist — Exact Opposite of Jesus Christ

We have seen previously that in theomatics, direct opposites can have the same theomatic values. The Greek transliteration of Gorbachev's name gives us the following:

Mikhail S. Gorbachev
Μιχαηλ Σ. Γορμβαχοβ' equals 888 X 2, or 111 X 16

And: Gorbachev
Γορμβαχοβ equals 888, or 111 X 8

Let us now see whether this theomatic value carries through the other transliterations of his name. In Russian again:

Mikhail S. Gorbachev
МИХАИЛ С. ГОРБАЧЕВ''' equals 111 X 12

And in Hebrew: Mikhail Sergeevich Gorbachev
מיכאל סצרגייןזיטש גארביטטששאןן equals 111 X 12

The Probability of This

The probability of any one man's name giving us these theomatic values in Russian and Greek has been calculated. Because of the many possible variations of the transliteration in Hebrew, these values were not included. If they had been, the number would be very much higher.

The probability of Gorbachev's name giving us the theomatic values in Russian and Greek which are functions of the numbers 666, 46, 111 and 888 is one in:

318,300,604,672!

2

The Beast From the Sea

It is so stupid of modern civilization to have given up believing in Satan when he is the only explanation of it. (Ronald Knox)

The heart of a man is the place the devils dwell in: I feel sometimes a hell within myself. (Sir Thomas Browne)

Revelation 13:1 tells us, "And I stood upon the sands of the sea, and saw a beast rise up out of the sea...."

This is how John describes the appearance of the antichrist in his vision of the end times. One moment the sea was calm and tranquil and then the beast bursts upon the scene — suddenly and unexpectedly.

This is exactly how Mikhail Gorbachev appeared upon the world scene — suddenly and unexpectedly. On March 11, 1985, Konstantin Chernenko died quite abruptly and a man whose name was totally unknown to the majority of people in the rest of the world was named to be leader of the Soviet Union. Gorbachev burst upon the world scene in the same way as John's beast arose from the sea. One moment he was not there — then suddenly he burst from the depths of obscurity to head the Soviet Union and take command of the most powerful military force in history.

The beast which John describes is unquestionably the antichrist. No biblical scholar disputes this fact. But what is the significance of the sea from which he rises? Biblical prophecy, especially in the book of Revelation, is shrouded in symbolism. But I believe we can penetrate this symbolism and fit many pieces of the end-time puzzle together and see exactly what John's vision means for us today and in the immediate future.

For many Christians the events of this vision will culminate in eternal happiness, even though they may have to go through a time of great persecution and unparalleled troubles. But to many in the world, this picture of the end times may be terrifying. And for good reason, for it will bring to them the beginning of everlasting torment and unspeakable horror.

The Sea

You have undoubtedly heard the expression that could be used to describe a public speaker, for example, looking out on 'a sea of faces.' A multitude of people may be described as 'a sea of people.' I believe this is exactly what is meant by the sea from which the beast arises. It is possible that the 'sea' from which Gorbachev has so abruptly risen is the great mass of people which make up the Soviet Union. He has risen from the 'Russian sea.'

Another clue was given in the Associated Press story which announced the selection of Mikhail S. Gorbachev by the Politburo as General Secretary of the Soviet Communist Party. The population of the Soviet Union was given, and you will recognize that particular number from the last chapter where we dealt with Theomatics.

The population of the Soviet Union was 276 million when Mikhail Gorbachev was named leader of the Soviet Union. 276 is Satan's number. Gorbachev, therefore, arose from Satan's Sea.

Satan's Power

Revelation 13:2 reads, "...and the dragon gave him his power, his seat, and great authority."

If Satan had no power, there would be no trouble in the world. His power is certainly no match for God's power, but it is considerable nonetheless. Paul, in Second Corinthians 4:4, calls Satan 'the god of this world.'

Satan tempted Jesus by making him an offer of all the kingdoms of the world if only He would worship the devil. God has allowed Satan to have temporary dominion over the earth and the power to destroy those who have fallen victim to his temptations. Everything Satan touches he destroys.

Satan has the power to be a convincing liar, and many have believed his lies. Even in the paradise of the Garden of Eden, Eve fell victim to his ability to lie in a convincing manner. God had forbidden them from eating of the fruit of the Tree of Knowledge of Good and Evil.

God said, "But of the tree of knowledge of good and evil, thou shalt not eat of it: for in the day that thou eatest thereof thou shalt surely die" (Gen. 2:17).

But Satan, the serpent, lied to Eve and convinced her. "And the serpent said unto the woman, Ye shall not surely die" (Gen. 3:4).

Ever since Eve believed the lie of Satan, people have gone on believing his lies — and being destroyed in the process. Satan has great power, and he will give this power to his agent on earth — the antichrist.

Mikhail S. Gorbachev is indisputably one of the most powerful men in the world today. As General Secretary of the Soviet Communist Party, he is also the commander-in-chief of the most potent armed forces the world has ever seen. At his word thousands of intercontinental ballistic missiles could be fired from their concrete silos and mobile launchers, carrying sufficient megatons of nuclear destruction to annihilate the population of the world many times over.

Under his control are not only the people of the Soviet Union, but also the people and the armed forces of the countries of the Soviet bloc nations who live under communism and whose lives are totally controlled by their communist masters.

No dissent is tolerated in these countries. There is a wry joke circulated among the people of the Soviet Union which says, "Of course there is freedom of speech behind the Iron Curtain today. Any citizen is free to say whatever he wants to ...*once!*"

Satan's Seat

President Ronald Reagan had called the Soviet Union 'an evil empire,' and he was perfectly correct to do so. It *is* an evil empire. The state religion is atheism. The avowed aims of the Soviet Union include world domination and the eradication of all forms of genuine worship of God from the face of the earth. It is a system which encourages its leaders to lie, to cheat, to mislead, to use any form of deception or deceit to further its aim and achieve its objectives.

Many scholars have looked for a revival of the Roman Empire and the subsequent rise of the antichrist from this. But a look at international politics and power today should convince anyone that the revival of the Roman Empire as it was at the time of Jesus is impossible. The states which made up the once-powerful Rome are in absolutely no position to dominate the world, which is what the antichrist and his seat of power will do.

Others have postulated that the European Common Market will be the power base from which the antichrist will arise, stating that this is the "revived Roman Empire." Again, a brief examination of these countries should preclude this.

I have heard some say that the antichrist must be a Jew; others say he will be a Syrian, but there is no basis in Revelation prophecy for these statements. These come from those who have misinterpreted Daniel 8. The sum total of the antichrist prophecy is contained in John's book of the Revelation, with some supporting Scriptures from the Old and New Testaments. All of the clues for recognizing this agent of Satan, however, are contained in the Revelation prophecy.

What country would be most capable of taking total control of the world, either by fomenting internal revolution or by direct military action? If Satan chose to reside in one nation, which do you believe he would choose?

Most would answer these questions, without hesitation, by identifying the Soviet Union. I believe we may safely call the Soviet Union 'Satan's Seat' of power today.

And would not this avowed atheistic state which has the most powerful military force ever assembled — both nuclear and conventional — be the perfect power base for the antichrist to launch his campaign for world conquest?

Gorbachev is sitting in that very seat of power. He is sitting in Satan's seat.

We found in the last chapter that the Cyrillic alphabet was a numerical language. We found that Gorbachev's name was a function of 666, 46, and 111. Could other Russian words give us clues to whether or not the Soviet Union is truly Satan's seat of power and the country from which the antichrist will launch his attack upon the world?

To determine this, let's examine a few Russian words. We will use the numerical values of the Cyrillic alphabet as shown in the chart in Exhibit II.

| Russia | Россия | Russia equals 666 x 8 |
| God | Бог | God equals 66 |

Could it be that in the end times, the god (66) of Russia (666 x 8) will be the antichrist (666), Mikhail S. Gorbachev?

Let's look now at a name for Russia, the Soviet Union. Using a Russian language dictionary, we find that grammatically these words 'Soviet' and 'Union' are spelled:

Soviet Union   СОВЕТСКИЙ СОI-ОЗ

But in each case, the dictionary gives the first spelling of the word 'Soviet' as:

Soviet   СОВЕТ

When we use this spelling in conjunction with the Russian word for union, we find and interesting theomatic revelation:

| Soviet Union | СОВЕТ СОI-ОЗ | equals 276 x 16, and 46 x 96 |

Could it be any clearer? The Soviet Union *is* Satan's seat of power and the dragon (Satan) has given the antichrist his power, his seat, and great authority; just as the Revelation prophecy has warned us.

Satan's Authority

Ephesians 6:12 tells us, "For we wrestle not against flesh and blood, but against principalities, against powers, against the rulers of the darkness of this world, against spiritual wickedness in high places."

Satan has been given the power to corrupt the governments of the world, to deceive multitudes of people, to foster cults and false religions which blind people to the truth that salvation can come only through God's Son, Jesus Christ. (See John 4:16.)

Satan will give this authority to his human agent of world conquest, the antichrist. This man will speak words of peace, words of hope, words describing the possibility of great things. But just as the serpent lied to Eve, those who believe his lies will be led to utter and everlasting destruction.

Mikhail S. Gorbachev is talking about peace. He is offering a plan for nuclear disarmament. His seat of power allows him to make these offers to a world threatened by nuclear holocaust. But Paul spoke of these very times when he told of those in the world in the end times, before the return of Jesus Christ: "For when they shall say, Peace and safety; then sudden destruction cometh upon them, as travail upon a woman with child..." (1 Thess. 4:3).

The Soviet Definition of Peace

To the western mind, peace is a time of tranquility, a time when nations cooperate with one another, when there is no war between countries. But the communist definition is not the same as ours. To a communist, peace is a time of achieving what cannot be won by hostilities. It is a time to gain an upper hand, *a time of preparation for war.*

In his book, *You Can Trust the Communists (To Do Exactly As They Say)* [1], Dr. Fred Schwarz describes the communist definition of peace:

"The Communists believe they are at war. They desire 'peace' with all their hearts. But to them, peace is that golden consummation when the progressive force of Communism totally overwhelms American imperialism and climaxes in Communist world conquest. By definition, 'peace' is Communist world conquest."

Unfortunately, very few Americans speak Russian. if we did, perhaps we all could better see just what this atheistic force which has been let loose upon the world actually is saying and doing. On the subject of 'peace,' I want to share with you exactly what Gorbachev and his evil empire are saying when they say, "I want peace."

Let's look at this Russian word for peace.

МИР is the Russian word for 'peace.'
But МИР is also the Russian word for 'world.'

How much clearer must it be? When Gorbachev says, "I want peace," he is really saying, "I want the world!"

But Why Russia?

How did Russia become Satan's sea? What happened to this land and its people to allow Satan to find a base for his evil operations? To find an answer, we must look briefly at Russian history.

The people of the Soviet Union are a conglomeration of many ethnic groups and nationalities. The Soviet Union is far from being a homogeneous country.

Within a land mass consisting of one-sixth of the earth's land, a mixture of over one hundred different ethnic groups lives.

The Slavic people make up the single largest portion of the population, about one-half the total. The second largest group is the Ukranians, followed by the Byelorussians. Smaller groups make up the remainder. Armenians and Georgians in the south; Asiatic Yukuts, Buryats and Tuvans in Siberia; and the Chukchi in the Russian Aleutian Islands who are closely related to the Eskimos of North America.

The vast majority of the people of the Soviet Union are honest, hard-working, decent and gentle folks. They do not want war any more than Americans want war. The majority are not even Communist Party members, who make up only about nine percent of the Soviet population. Their situation has been forced on them and they are powerless to do anything about it.

How then did Satan take control of this land? How did the yoke of communism envelop these people? Why don't they rise up and throw off this evil and oppressive government? Why don't they demand their freedom?

The Russian people *have never experienced true freedom*. Throughout their history, they have been under the heel of one ruthless, cruel ruler after another. They were ripe for a communist takeover because *at the time it seemed much better than what they had*.

Communism is not a Russian invention. Its founders, Karl Marx and Friedrich Engels, were Germans. The ideology had to be imported into Russia, and it was only because the time was exactly right for a military takeover that it succeeded at all.

The Communists Steal a Revolution

The early years of the 1900s brought a series of revolts against the Czar and his ruling class. These revolts were simply uprisings of common people who had been brought to this extreme measure by the oppression of the wealthy landowners.

The Czar fought off these revolts and the beginning of World War I brought a temporary interruption of the people's rebellion. But in 1917, and by the end of the war, events exploded into full-scale revolution. The Bolsheviks muscled into leadership positions, and with only a minority of members, were able to steal the revolution away from the common people.

For the Russian people, any hope of freedom was quickly snatched away as they exchanged one form of tyranny for another. The trickle of blood by which the Czars had maintained power became a raging torrent under the Bolsheviks as Vladimir Ilyich Lenin began to purge Russia from all sources of dissent. All other political parties were outlawed, and in what was supposed to be a 'worker's paradise,' all labor unions were abolished. When the newspapers were taken over by the Communist Party, the truth was quickly exchanged for propaganda and lies published by Lenin and his cohorts.

In 1918 Lenin issued a proclamation urging the 'purge of all kinds of harmful insects from Russia.' These 'harmful insects' turned out to be all 'class enemies,' such as all land or home owners, former civil servants, all members of parish councils, all priests, monks and nuns, and even those who had sung in church choirs. In addition, all those who had received any type of university training were purged, including the doctors, engineers, teachers, and agricultural experts. What happened was that the very people who could have built a stable and thriving economic system and a modern, twentieth-century society were either killed outright or wasted in Siberian labor camps. The communist leaders were for the most part uneducated ruffians whose hands dripped with the blood of the very people who could have contributed the most to this new country, the Soviet Union.

Solzhenitsyn tells of the millions of Russians who were 'flushed down the sewage disposal system' in his chilling book, *The Gulag Archipelago* [2], in the blood-letting that began in 1917 and continued throughout the regimes of both Lenin and Stalin, ceasing only in 1953 when Stalin died.

During this time entire villages were uprooted and moved to the frozen tundra of Siberia. There they were unloaded from cattle cars, and abandoned with only the few pieces of clothing they had brought in their cardboard suitcases. They had no tools, no shelter, no food, and no means of survival; they were left to die of exposure or starvation in the frigid Siberian winter. The populations of some ethnic groups were almost wiped out.

Tens of millions of other 'enemies of the state' were either executed or sent to forced labor camps for sentences of from five to twenty-five years. All of the major public works projects built during this time, such as dams, canals, electrical generating plants, and even factories, were constructed by these slave laborers. Because these people died quickly and new labor was needed, local police were given quotas which they had to fill from the citizens who were 'under their protection.' After the true criminals had been rounded up and the quota still had not been met, the police arrested anyone at all to make up the body count that was required, whether that person was guilty of a crime or not. Only the suspicion of holding anti-state opinions was necessary for a five-year sentence to a labor camp or 'rehabilitation' in the Urals or Siberia.

It has been estimated that at least ten times the number of Russian citizens have been exterminated in this manner than all those who died in Hitler's death camps during World War II. Never in the course of history have any people been so savagely treated by their own government as have the people of the Soviet Union and the Soviet bloc nations.

What more could Satan have asked for? History has seen the rise of many cruel empires, but even in these barbaric states, citizen's rights were respected. These empires were not atheistic societies in the true sense, for they all had religions although most of these religions were centered on pagan gods and idols. But even the worst of these retained some sense of morality and personal ethics. None embraced the pure, unadulterated atheism of communism, nor conducted their internal and external affairs with the utter lack of decency and honesty as the Soviet Union has and does.

Satan has indeed found a home within the thick walls and the high towers of the Kremlin.

What Do We Know About Gorbachev?

Mikhail S. Gorbachev's rise to power was so swift, so sudden, that it caught the world by surprise. Few had ever heard his name before.

He was born on March 2, 1931, in the small village of Privolnoye in the Stavropol region of the Caucasus to a family of peasants. His father was a machine operator and served in the army during the war. He died in 1976. His mother still lives in Privolnoye.

He studied law in Moscow and in 1952 he joined the Communist Party. After graduation he returned to Stavropol and was appointed First Secretary of the district Communist Party at age 39. He remained a low-ranking member in a backwoods town until his fortunes changed abruptly.

In 1978 his meteoric rise began when he was named head of the agricultural branch of the Central Committee Secretariat in Moscow and was responsible for the day-to-day operation of the Soviet agricultural system. Apparently it made no difference that he was a lawyer and had absolutely no training in agriculture.

Even Soviet crop failures would not hinder his advancement, for just a year later, in 1979, he became a candidate member of the Politburo, the highest governmental group in the Soviet Union. In October, 1982, he was made a full Politburo member.

After serving only four-and-a-half years in the Politburo, he was named General Secretary of the Soviet Communist Party and supreme leader of the Soviet Union and chief of the most powerful military force ever assembled.

How did this man rise so quickly in a society where it is common for men to serve twenty-five or thirty years within the party framework before reaching even a middle-rank position? Was his unprecedented elevation a result of demonstrated skill and leadership qualities? What propelled him to the top in such a short space of time? Who was responsible for his selection to the Central Committee over an estimated 2,000 men of similar education and background? Why was he named to the office of Politburo candidate after only one year in Moscow? Who is responsible for all this? There can be only one answer! Satan was responsible!

Revelation 13 tells us more about the beast: "And the beast which I saw was like unto a leopard, and his feet were as the feet of a bear, and his mouth as the mouth of a lion...."

Like a Leopard

Funk and Wagnalls Standard Reference Encyclopedia has this to say about a leopard, "It is fiercer than a tiger, often attacking a man without provocation." A leopard is known for its cunning and cruelty. It will wait in ambush for unsuspecting prey. It is not particular about what it kills. It will eat anything.

The communist ideology which has shaped every Soviet leader since Lenin has these very same characteristics, and Gorbachev is a product of that ideology. Instead of truth and openness there is trickery and deceit. Communism has consumed every nation which has relaxed its guard, using internal subversion as well as overt military force.

It totally destroys all people who fall into its clutches, drinking their lifeblood. Gorbachev has the cunning of a leopard. His classmates in law school in Moscow remember him as, "...a flamboyant little fellow who loved to flaunt his knowledge of the official party line...." He has charmed the West with his charismatic personality and smile, but behind the smiling face are the teeth and claws of a leopard.

A Bear's Feet

The bear is readily recognized as the symbol of Russia. Gorbachev's feet, his roots, are in peasant Russia from which he rose so suddenly to power.

The bear is known for its strength. It is a carnivorous animal, killing and eating the flesh of its prey. Gorbachev's feet are indeed the feet of a bear, a strong Russian bear.

A Lion's Mouth

When a lion roars, the whole jungle stops and listens. The lion is called "the king of the beasts." Certainly, the beast which John saw rising from the sea will be the 'king' of beasts, for he will be the most powerful and deadly animal ever seen in history.

When the leader of the Soviet Union speaks, he has the world's attention. The international press reports to the world every remark he utters in public and the nations of the earth ponder his every statement to try to see just how it affects them. Gorbachev's mouth can certainly be likened to the mouth of a lion, a powerful and deadly lion.

Revelation 12:3 tells us, "And there appeared another wonder in heaven; and behold a great red dragon, having seven heads and ten horns, and seven crowns upon his heads."

A RED dragon. RED is the symbolic color of communism. The RED army is the Soviet army. The RED star is a communist symbol. The RED dragon in John's vision is Satan.

The population of the Soviet Union was 276 million when Gorbachev came into power. Satan's number is 276.

An article appearing in the newspaper shortly after the selection of Mikhail S. Gorbachev by the Politburo, as General Secretary of the Soviet Communist Party, also told of the Soviet SS-20 missiles which are aimed at the major cities of Western Europe. How many of these SS-20 missiles were there at this time? There were 276 of them. Again we see Satan's number.

3

The Ten Kingdoms and the Ten Kings

The dictatorship of the Communist Party is maintained by recourse to every form of violence. (Leon Trotsky)

Socialism is workable only in heaven where it isn't needed and in hell where they've already got it. (Cecil Palmer)

Although much of the Revelation prophecy is given in symbolism, there are times when prophetic information is explained very clearly to us in the Scriptures. This is the case with the ten kingdoms and the ten kings described in John's vision of the beast from the sea.

Revelation 13:1 describes the appearance of the beast: "And I stood upon the sand of the sea, and saw a beast rise up out of the sea, having seven heads and ten horns, and upon his horns ten crowns, and upon his heads the name of blasphemy."

Crowns usually denote kingdoms and John tells us this is exactly what the crowns do represent. Revelation 17:12 makes it very clear: "And the ten horns which thou sawest are ten kings, which have received no kingdom as yet; but receive power as kings one hour with the beast."

We are told that the ten crowns are ten kings, and that they will depend strictly on the antichrist for their power to rule. They will be in power for only a short time, probably only as long as the antichrist is in power. This is indicated by the term 'one hour,' which in prophecy does not mean a literal hour, but a short space of time.

Does this picture fit our candidate, Mikhail S. Gorbachev? Yes, in fact Gorbachev fulfills this part of the Revelation prophecy in two distinctly different ways.

When he assumed leadership of the Soviet Union on March 11,

1985, Gorbachev became not only General Secretary of the Soviet Communist Party and leader of the Soviet Union; he also became the absolute leader of all the Soviet bloc countries. These countries — and their leaders — have no power of their own, but only that which the Soviet Union and Gorbachev allow them to have.

At one time, each of the Soviet bloc countries were independent nations, but World War II and the unfortunate treaties which resulted from that conflict gave the Soviet Union control over them.

The first three nations are:

1. Latvia
2. Estonia
3. Lithuania

These small nations existed as free and independent political entities before World War II. Unfortunately, being small and militarily weak, they were used as pawns by both Hitler and Stalin. As a result of a treaty between these two dictators, German troops marched into and occupied half of Poland, while Russian troops occupied eastern Poland, as well as Latvia, Estonia and Lithuania.

These three small nations had signed mutual assistance pacts with the Soviet Union. Mutual assistance, to the Soviet way of thinking, means total domination. They have all lost their independent national identities and political sovereignty and you will not find them on any map of Europe today. All have been absorbed into the Soviet Union. But no western nation has ever recognized the Soviet Union's absorption of them and they still retain governments in exile.

At the end of hostilities in 1945, Soviet troops occupied much of Eastern Europe. Along with Russian soldiers there were political organizers who quickly formed small communist parties within the occupied lands. Stalin made the mistake of allowing Austrians to vote in free and honest elections, feeling confident that they would elect communist party members. He was wrong. The Austrians did not elect a single communist. Stalin did not repeat that mistake. In the other occupied countries, the elections were tightly controlled and the guns of the Soviet troops made certain that the people voted in favor of the communist candidates for office. All of these nations emerged as vassals of the Soviet Union after World War II:

  4. Poland
  5. Czechoslovakia
  6. Hungary
  7. Romania
  8. East Germany
  9. Bulgaria

But something is wrong! These total only nine! There should be ten nations to fulfill the prophecy.

Although the absorption of these nine nations at the conclusion of World War II would set the stage for the appearance of the antichrist, the time was not yet right. The tenth kingdom was not to be added until the end of 1979 when Brezhnev ordered the invasion of Afghanistan. This is the tenth kingdom and we will see how this contributes to the fulfillment of another prophecy concerning the antichrist in a later chapter.

Our list is now complete. The tenth nation is Afghanistan.

With a hand-picked man in Kabul (the capital of Afghanistan), the Soviet Union controls the major portion of this barren and desolate country. Although resistance continues in the countryside, the Soviets control the cities and are doing exactly what they invaded this country to accomplish. They are constructing two large military bases along the very strategic border with Iran. The antichrist will use these later to fulfill additional end-times prophecy.

Ten Kings

The prophecy concerning the ten crowns and ten kings has been fulfilled by the ten nations which are completely controlled by the Kremlin and the Soviet leader, but this prophecy has been fulfilled doubly in another most interesting way.

When Brezhnev ordered the invasion of Afghanistan, he did something else as well. The Politburo had traditionally been composed of eleven members. The Afghan war was not popular with other high-ranking Soviet officials and it was apparent that Brezhnev had made a serious miscalculation. There was even talk about this causing Brezhnev's political demise.

Brezhnev countered this threat to his leadership by changing both the composition and number of members of the Politburo, enlarging it to fourteen instead of the traditional eleven. He stacked it with loyal friends.

But even Brezhnev was not immune to the KGB and its chief, Yuri Andropov. There had always been corruption on high levels within the Soviet Union and the other Communist bloc countries, and this had been considered one of the 'perks' of the elite. But the Gierek regime in Poland collapsed when the blatant corruption was publicly exposed. This corruption had been so extensive that the scandal reached into the Kremlin and this did not go unnoticed by Brezhnev's political enemies. A picture of what occurred at this time is given in *Andropov*, by Zhores A. Medvedev [1].

A resolution was passed in September of 1980 by the Central Committee of the Soviet Communist Party against official corruption. It stated that corrupt officials should be removed from office and exposed, *regardless of their positions*. The KGB would, of course, be involved in any investigation of alleged wrongdoing.

With the politically ambitious Andropov at the helm of the KGB, the investigations were not long in coming. Foreign newsmen were the recipients of 'leaks' from official sources concerning investigations in progress which involved Brezhnev's daughter, Galina Churbanov, and her third husband, General Yuri Churbanov, who was Deputy Minister of Internal Affairs.

This startling investigation involved the smuggling of diamonds abroad, currency speculation, and bribery. Also involved were the director of the Soviet national circus and his wife who were close friends of Brezhnev's daughter. It was said that when the police searched their apartment they found over $200,000 in currency and over one million dollars worth of diamonds and other precious stones. Brezhnev's son, Yuri, who was elected to the Central Committee of the Communist Party in 1981, was also linked to this scandal. Galina Brezhneva-Churbanova was taken to a Moscow hospital with what

was described as a 'nervous breakdown.' No high party official
wanted her to be charged, of course, or to be a witness in any trial.
There were too many closets full of skeletons to allow her to do that
and too many other high party officials who might be dragged in with
her.

Almost immediately there were quite a few 'suicides' among highly
placed party and government men. But this was only the beginning of
Andropov's investigation into official corruption. On March 7, 1982,
one of Europe's largest newspapers ran a headline, "KGB LEADS
ATTACK ON BREZHNEV MAFIA."

Konstantin Chernenko was the heir-apparent to succeed Brezhnev.
During Brezhnev's infrequent absences, he served as Chairman of the
Secretariat. But Chernenko's close ties with Brezhnev also made him
very vulnerable in the event the Soviet leader fell from power as a
result of scandal. Andropov's intent was to see that this was exactly
what would happen.

Early in 1982 Andropov placed the documented case against
Brezhnev's daughter and the others on the desk of Mikhail Suslov. The
Soviet criminal code was very specific in such cases. The penalty
would be death. Suslov immediately knew that this would mean
Brezhnev's downfall, and possibly his own. He also knew that within
the KGB Brezhnev had an ally, First Deputy Chairman General
Semyon Tsvigun, Brezhev's brother-in-law and an old friend from the
post-war days. He knew that Tsvigun was totally loyal to the Soviet
leader.

Suslov could not ignore the documents which Andropov had placed
before him, but decided not to act on it until he had spoken personally
with Tsvigun to determine whether anything could be done to squelch
this explosive case.

There was apparently a heated argument between Suslov and
Tsvigun which ended by Suslov telling the Deputy Chairman that he
would be expelled from the party if he allowed such a case to become
public. The next day Tsvigun was found dead, apparently a suicide
—but his obituary notice was signed only by KGB officials and not by
any members of the Politburo.

Suslov was so upset by the whole affair that he suffered a stroke and died a few days later. On the morning of Suslov's funeral, the KGB moved to make arrests. Kolevatov, the director of the National Circus, and his wife were taken into custody along with several other suspects in the case. Since all of the members of the Politburo were attending Suslov's funeral, there was no one available to interfere.

It was later rumored that Kolevatov and another man were dead, one by suicide and the other with a heart attack. Soon after, Brezhnev's son-in-law was dismissed from his post as Deputy Minister of Internal Affairs and sent to a minor position in Murmansk.

On November 10, 1982, Brezhnev died from what was announced as a heart attack. As is usual under such conditions, an alert was sounded and the two Soviet divisions which are quartered in the Moscow suburbs made ready to move into the city if needed. All KGB employees and all policemen were ordered to remain at their posts at the end of the working day. When the second shifts reported for work, there was twice the normal complement of both KGB and police on duty.

An emergency meeting of the Politburo was called. When this highest body of the Soviet Union had assembled, Red Army Marshal D.F. Ustinov arose and looked sternly at the men seated around the polished table. He then proposed that Yuri Andropov be elected General Secretary of the Soviet Communist Party and head of the country. No one objected, not even Chernenko, who knew that with the Red Army supporting Andropov he had no chance.

One of the Politburo members seated around the table was Mikhail S. Gorbachev, Soviet Agricultural Secretary. He was a close associate of Andropov and when the man took sick almost immediately after assuming office, it was Gorbachev who was the liaison between the General Secretary and the Politburo.

Fifteen months later Andropov died. There was another hurried meeting of the Politburo. But when the announcement of Andropov's successor was made, everyone was shocked. It was Konstantin Chernenko who emerged as General Secretary and leader of the

Soviet Union. He was another man who was dying on his feet (from emphysema), and we will see later just how this fits in with the antichrist prophecy.

Chernenko, at seventy-two years of age, was the oldest man ever to head the Soviet Union and he lived for only thirteen months after assuming that role. Now was Gorbachev's time, and again the Politburo met. But how many members were present?

Brezhnev had enlarged this body to fourteen members, but death and attrition had reduced this number back to eleven, including Gorbachev. No one had been appointed to fill the vacancies.

The remaining *ten* members of the Politburo elected Mikhail S. Gorbachev as General Secretary of the Soviet Communist Party. Ten members, kings who have no kingdoms of their own but who serve by the consent of the leader of the Soviet Union, appointed the General Secretary of the Soviet Communist Party.

Revelation 17:13 tells us about these men, "These have one mind, and shall give their power and strength to the beast."

Certainly the ten Politburo members were of one mind — the aims and objectives of world communism and the domination of the world by the Soviet Union. They have given their strength and power to Gorbachev.

This portion of the antichrist prophecy had been filled in double measure. There are ten nations under direct control of the Soviet Union. These are led by Soviet puppets who are of one mind, to serve the leader of the Soviet Union.

The ten members of the Politburo give their power and strength to Gorbachev. Our candidate for the antichrist can certainly claim ten crowns, just as the Revelation prophecy has told us.

4

The Seven Heads

The created world is but a small parenthesis in eternity. (Sir Thomas Browne)

The souls of emperors and cobblers are cast in the same mold. The same reason that makes us wrangle with a neighbor causes a war betwixt princes. (Montaigne)

As we begin this chapter, let us refer again to John's description of the beast: "And I stood upon the sand of the sea, and saw a beast rise up out of the sea, having seven heads and ten horns, and upon his horns ten crowns, and upon his heads the name of blasphemy" (Rev. 13:1).

The beast has seven heads and upon these heads is written a blasphemous name. What is connected with the leader of the Soviet Union and corresponds to these seven heads? What is the blasphemous name?

A beast's danger lies in his weapons: his claws and teeth. The head of a beast contains the teeth that are used to consume his prey. The teeth are usually the most dangerous part of the beast, for without them he could not eat and live, and without them he would pose no real threat to others.

The Soviet Union has seven such heads. They are the Warsaw Pact nations:

The Seven Heads of the Beast
1. The Soviet Union
2. Poland
3. Czechoslovakia
4. Hungary
5. Romania
6. Bulgaria
7. East Germany

If Mikhail S. Gorbachev is truly the antichrist, these nations and their armed forces are the tools by which he will attempt to impose Satan's will upon the entire world. The armed might of these nations stands ready, behind the Iron Curtain, poised to attack when the antichrist gives the order. In addition to their armed forces, these nations all have intelligence operations similar to the KGB and a large contingent of covert agents operating throughout the free world. These agents, in addition to gathering secret information, are ready to begin a highly integrated plan of subversion and sabotage when the order is given from the Kremlin.

In the nations of the free world where the Warsaw Pact nations maintain embassies or consulates, at least half of the personnel attached to these diplomatic missions are actively engaged in espionage for their communist-controlled governments.

The satellite nations all give their strength to the Soviet Union and they have a powerful military force. In addition to the Soviet strength of over four million active-duty military personnel, the other Warsaw Pact countries increase the combined military strength by about one million and have an estimated trained reserve of another two million. These communist countries also have a para-military force of over six hundred thousand, which gives the total number of armed forces at Gorbachev's command as follows:

Active-duty military, 5 million

Active-duty para-military, 1.2 million

Trained reserves, 7.2 million

The Warsaw Pact could quickly field a force of nearly fourteen million troops. To put this into perspective, during World War II the United States mobilized a force of about sixteen million men, but this took almost five years to accomplish. The Soviet Union and the Warsaw Pact nations could do this in a very short period of time.

The Soviet strategic nuclear force is awesome, capable of destroying the entire population of the world several times over. It is believed that the Soviets do not allow the other members of the Warsaw Pact to possess nuclear arms, for the fear of rebellion is always present in the paranoid Soviet mind. The Soviet force consists of at least:

    1,398 Land-Based ICBMs
    981 Submarine-Based ICBMs

This is a total of at least 2,379 delivery vehicles, the majority of which carry multiple warheads. This does not include intermediate-range weapons such as SS-20's whose targets include European and Chinese sites, such as cities and military installations.

The Soviet Air Force is estimated to have at least 4,500 bombers capable of delivering nuclear bombs or air-to-surface nuclear missiles, with ranges of from 1,100 to 14,000 miles. From Siberian bases, even the medium-range aircraft could reach U.S. cities and strategic targets.

Poised just beyond the Iron Curtain are an estimated 35,000 Soviet and Warsaw Pact tanks. This fast-moving armor could overrun most of Europe within a few weeks, were it not for the West's nuclear deterrent. Although NATO conventional forces are strong, no military commander expects the NATO force to be capable of stopping the Soviet armor with only conventional weapons.

The armed might of the Soviet and Warsaw Pact nations are the teeth of the beast's heads. And they are formidable teeth, indeed.

The Heads of the Red Dragon

We have seen before that Satan — pictured as a great red dragon —appeared in John's vision of the end times. "And there appeared another wonder in heaven; and behold a great red dragon, having seven heads and ten horns, and seven crowns upon his heads" (Rev. 12:3).

These seven heads and seven crowns which Satan, the dragon, wears are also the seven Warsaw Pact nations. If his agent on earth, the antichrist, can wear these heads and crowns, then certainly his master — Satan — may also claim them. The ten horns are the ten kings who have given their power and strength to the antichrist and his master, Satan.

The Name of Blasphemy

Revelation 13:1, "...and upon his heads the name of blasphemy."

Webster defines the word 'blasphemy' as follows: "profane or contemptuous speech, writing or action concerning God or anything held as divine."

Communism is most contemptuous of God in speech, writing and action. The seven Warsaw Pact nations are under communist rule, authority and ideology. Their leaders are all communists. Their schools indoctrinate their children in communism. To a dedicated communist there is no God but the state. To a Warsaw Pact communist, the leader of the Soviet Union is God.

Communism, itself, is blasphemy against God. This is the word (communism) which is indelibly written on the seven heads of the beast. This name is written on all of the seven Warsaw Pact nations.

Believe it or not, the Soviet Constitution guarantees its citizens the right to freedom of religion. The Soviet Penal Code makes it a criminal offense to interfere with a person's freedom of religion. The Soviet Union was one of the thirty-five nations which signed the Helsinki Final Act, which states:

> Participating governments will respect human rights and fundamental freedoms, including the freedom of thought, conscience, religion, or belief....Within this framework partic- ipating states will recognize and respect the freedom of the individual to profess and practice alone or in community with others, religion or belief and acting in accordance with the dictates of his own conscience....
>
> (Paragraph 7)

In practice, however, it is quite a different situation. Under communist regimes, Bibles and other religious publications are confiscated. Likewise, it is illegal for one to testify to another person about his faith. Children under the age of eighteen cannot attend church and no one including their own parents, may legally teach them anything about religion. The only clergymen who are permitted to hold services are those who are in the employ of the state, and these clerics must preach only what the state allows them to preach. The official state religion of atheism is taught to all children in the public schools, and the state confines those they label to be 'religious fanatics' to mental institutions. Does this sound like freedom of religion?

The Deadly Wound

Revelation 13:3, "And I saw one of his heads as it were wounded to death; and his deadly wound was healed: and all the world wondered after the beast."

This part of the prophecy has not yet been fulfilled. It is not possible to predict the exact meaning of this portion of the antichrist prophecy, but knowing what is meant by the beast's heads, we can make an educated guess as to what will happen when this part of the prophecy is fulfilled.

John saw one of the beast's heads with a serious wound, a wound which was likely to cause the death of the beast. The nature of this deadly wound is described in Revelation 13:14: "...that they should make an image to the beast, which had the wound by a sword, and did live."

The wound was by a sword. In other words, it was a wound caused by warfare, by fighting. Since we know that "the heads of the beast" is a phrase referring to the Warsaw Pact nations, it would seem probable that this wound means that one of these nations will revolt against the Soviet Union. To describe the wound as deadly, almost causing the death of the antichrist — or his political downfall — makes it seem that it indicates that this rebellion will be successful, at least initially.

The continuing war in Afghanistan is certainly placing stress on the Soviet Union, but since it was Brezhnev who started this war and the last two Soviet leaders were not able to bring it to a close, it appears to be no real challenge to Gorbachev's leadership. Afghanistan is also not one of the 'heads' of the beast, because it is not part of the Warsaw Pact.

Although the continuing war in Afghanistan has recently been called 'a bleeding wound' by Gorbachev, it would seem more likely that the deadly wound to which John refers will be another, more potentially dangerous situation involving the rebellion of one of the Warsaw Pact nations.

In examining each of the Warsaw Pact nations: Poland, Czechoslovakia, Hungary, Romania, Bulgaria and East Germany, it would seem to me that Poland has the highest probability of internal unrest.

The Polish economy has been in dire straits for many years and the Poles have had the lowest standard of living of all the Soviet bloc nations. In late 1987 the Polish government held a national referendum on economic reform. The enactment of this reform would have meant higher prices for food and almost everything else the Poles must buy. This was rejected by an overwhelming vote by the Polish people.

Now the Polish government finds itself on the horns of a dilemma. In order for the Polish economy to survive, they will be forced to enact the very measures which were rejected by the people. There will be violent opposition to this and this may cause even more protest than the banning of Solidarity. Social upheaval, which always simmers just below the surface in Poland, may finally reach the boiling point.

Both Hungary and Czechoslovakia have attempted to defy Soviet power and each was crushed quickly under the heel of Soviet military might. In early 1968, the old-guard Stalinists in the Czech government were replaced by younger and more liberal men. Ludvik Svoboda became president and Alexander Dubcek took over the post of Secretary of the Czech Communist Party. The new cabinet pledged liberal reforms, both political and economic. The media, both press and radio, immediately took up this cause and became outspoken in their criticisms of the past and urged greater speed in implementing these reforms. Moscow insisted that the new regime slow down the pace of liberalization and in July the Politburo refused the demands of the Czech government for immediate reforms.

On August 21, 1968, Soviet, East German, Polish, Hungarian and Bulgarian troops, tanks and planes invaded Czechoslovakia. Dubcek and his cabinet were ousted and the Soviet-led occupation troops restored order and stopped the liberalization in its tracks. This was a warning to other Soviet bloc countries not to oppose their masters in the Kremlin.

There had been an earlier attempt by one of the Soviet satellites to throw off the communist yoke. In October of 1956 a revolt erupted in Budapest, Hungary, after the premier, Imre Nagy, and his cabinet, were ousted by the Hungarian Communist Party for 'anti-Marxism.' This had been instigated by Moscow.

The revolt forced the Hungarian communist leaders to flee the city and Nagy again took command of the government, announcing that there would be free elections and a two-party system. Hungarian freedom was short-lived. Two days later, Russian tanks and troops invaded and communist rule was forcibly restored. Nagy was executed.

But the dream of freedom cannot be forever stifled by guns and tanks. This wish for liberty remains in the hearts of the people of all the Warsaw Pact nations and only the presence of Soviet troops keeps these nations within the Soviet bloc. These people, unlike the Russians, have tasted the sweet wine of independence and freedom and a democratic way of life before they were imprisoned by the Soviet Union and communism.

But would another Warsaw Pact nation dare to rebel? Yes, I believe one would. Poland has been on the brink of open rebellion several times within the last few years. Just as the unplanned and spontaneous revolt in Hungary erupted suddenly, I believe that one day in the very near future there will be an incident in Poland which will push the Polish citizens beyond endurance. They will rise up against their Soviet masters with the pent-up rage of over forty years of enslavement and oppression.

The New York Times has reported that the Polish premier, Wojciech Jaruzelski, has already been summoned to Moscow by Gorbachev to discuss this boiling unrest in Poland. He received a stern warning — either smother this unrest or he will be removed from office and Soviet troops will do the job.

It will be necessary for the Polish communists to come down hard on the Roman Catholic clergy who continue to support Solidarity. But one more incident such as the murder of the popular Polish priest, Father Jerzy Popieluszko, by the Secret Police or if anything should happen to Lech Walesa, the leader of Solidarity, and the explosive situation in Poland could be instantly ignited into widespread revolt.

I do not believe the Polish army would fight against its own people, but would join in the revolt. The Polish army is a considerable fighting force, consisting of eight Motor Rifle Divisions, Five Tank Divisions and an Airborne Division. At the present time the Russians have only two Tank Divisions stationed on Polish soil.

If this is indeed what will be 'the deadly wound' of the Revelation prophecy, then it seems that the Poles would put up a heroic fight against the Soviet army. In fact, they would appear to actually be winning this war of independence. But Gorbachev would immediately invoke the 'Brezhnev Doctrine' which states that any problems within the Soviet bloc are to be considered 'internal affairs' and any nation that attempts to assist the revolting government would face Soviet retaliation. The free world would cheer on the valiant effort of the Poles, but would most likely be afraid to offer any aid.

The United States would be warned by the European nations not to interfere, afraid of possible Soviet action against them. Soviet rockets targeted on European cities will keep the West in terror of a nuclear war.

Gorbachev's political position will be jeopardized by the success of the Polish revolt. He will have to do something drastic or the success of the Poles will spark other captive nations also to revolt against the oppression of the Soviet Union. The Revelation prophecy tells us that this wound will be healed, and the world will be amazed at this healing. I believe the wording of this passage implies a healing of a very dramatic nature, one which the world does not foresee. I believe that in his desperation, Gorbachev might even use nuclear weapons against the Poles to crush their rebellion. And the world will be amazed — indeed, horrified — at this quick and brutal end of the courageous Polish nation.

Although this may not be the precise scenario of the 'deadly wound' and its sudden and dramatic healing, it is a definite possibility. Perhaps the revolt will come from another of the Warsaw Pact countries. Only time will reveal this, but since these nations are the 'heads' of the beast, and the 'deadly wound' will be by the sword, something like this will very possibly occur.

I also believe that at the time of the healing of the deadly wound, another end-times personality will come onto the world scene — the false prophet. I also believe that the healing of the deadly wound will begin the final countdown to the Battle of Armageddon, and the end of life on this earth as we know it.

At this final battle, Jesus Christ will return — and this time all will recognize Him for who He is — some with great joy, others with stark terror — for then there will be no more time and the final judgment will come for all.

5

The Eighth King

It is true that liberty is precious — so precious that it must be rationed. (Nikolai Lenin)

There is no structural organization of society which can bring about the Kingdom of God on earth, since all systems can be perverted by the selfishness of man. (William Temple)

"And there are seven kings: five are fallen, and one is, and the other is yet to come; and when he cometh, he must continue a short space. And the beast that was, and is not, even he is the eighth, and is of the seven, and goeth into perdition" (Rev. 17:10, 11).

The antichrist will be the eighth in a line of 'kings,' or leaders. He will be of the same ideology as the previous seven. If our candidate, Mikhail S. Gorbachev, is truly the antichrist, then in addition to meeting the other parts of the Revelation prophecy, he must be the eighth in the line of leaders of the Soviet Union.

The First "King" — Lenin

Before the revolution of 1917, there was no such nation as the Soviet Union, or more correctly, the Union of Soviet Socialist Republics. Prior to that date the land was known as Russia and the new name for this country (U.S.S.R.) did not exist.

In November of 1917 one man emerged as the leader of the new state and the undisputed first 'king' of the Soviet Union. He was Vladimir Ilyich Lenin, who is sometimes referred to as Nikolai Lenin, and whose original surname was Ulyanov.

Lenin was born in 1870 at Simbrisk, now called Ulyanovsk. His early education took place there. In 1887 his older brother, Alexander, was arrested and executed for his part in a plot to assassinate Czar Alexander III, and Lenin's attitude toward the government was formed at this time. In December of 1887, Lenin was expelled from the Kazan University for taking part in a student political meeting and he began to study the writings of Karl Marx, and joined an illegal Marxist underground group.

Later he matriculated at St. Petersburg University and received a law degree. His revolutionary career began; he joined a group which distributed communist literature among local factory workers. In 1895 he was arrested and imprisoned for fourteen months. Upon his release he was sent into exile to Siberia.

After returning from exile he went to Germany and Switzerland where he organized a clandestine revolutionary newspaper which was secretly distributed in Russia. In 1903 he led the Bolshevik faction of the Russian Social Democratic Party.

When the Czarist regime was overthrown in 1917, he tried to return to Russia but was refused permission to enter via England. But the German government, wanting to strengthen the faction within Russia opposed to continuing the war, allowed him to travel through its lines in a sealed train.

He immediately attacked the policy of the provisional Russian government, urging greater power to be given to the 'soviets' or people's councils. The Bolshevik party became progressively stronger and in November of 1917 the provisional government under Aleksandr Kerenski was overthrown. Lenin became the head of the new government.

Lenin at once began a purge of all opposition, and with a Communist Party membership of substantially less than one million, he succeeded in imposing his rule over the entire country. He maintained this iron grip by allowing no opposing voice of disagreement. In 1924 the new name of this nation was established as the Union of Soviet Socialist Republics. Lenin died in 1924 at Gorki, near Moscow. He was the first 'king' of the newly formed Soviet Union.

The Second "King" — Stalin

At Lenin's death there was a power struggle between Joseph Stalin who was head of the Soviet Communist Party and Leon Trotsky, who was the Soviet Foreign Minister and commander of the Red Army. Stalin won and Trotsky went into exile in 1927. Trotsky was later assassinated by one of Stalin's agents in the suburbs of Mexico City, showing that Stalin's arm was long enough to reach half a world away.

Stalin not only continued Lenin's bloodbath against all opposition, but greatly increased it. Under Stalin, party members took control of all aspects of Soviet life, including the Red Army where the command of a trained military officer could be countermanded by a political commissar of lower rank and absolutely no military experience. This reign of terror continued until Stalin died in 1953. Joseph Stalin was the second 'king' of the Soviet Union.

The Third "King" — Malenkov

Upon Stalin's death, another power struggle took place among the ambitious men in the Kremlin. But they had all learned an important lesson —the bloodbaths had to cease. But before that was to be accomplished, one man would have to die or none of them would be safe.

Lavrenti Beria had been Stalin's most effective 'hatchet man.' As head of the Secret Police, he had been responsible for carrying out the bloody purges which the paranoid Stalin had ordered. Soon after Stalin's death, Beria was arrested and in December of 1953 it was announced that he and six accomplices had been found guilty of 'criminal and anti-state activities' and had been executed.

On March 6, 1953, immediately after Stalin's death, the Politburo announced the new leader of the Soviet Union. This was Georgi Maximilianovich Malenkov. He became both premier and Chairman of the Secretariat.

But there were many men whose ambitions had been thwarted under Stalin, and Malenkov faced immediate opposition, especially when he softened the hard line toward the west and tried to increase production of domestic goods at the expense of the military. His opponents used this against him and in February of 1956, they were successful in unseating him. Georgi Malenkov was the third 'king' of the Soviet Union.

The Fourth "King" — Krushchev

Nikita Sergeevich Krushchev had learned much from Joseph Stalin concerning where the real power lay in the Soviet Union. He knew that the man who controlled the Communist Party controlled the country; for the political commissars monitored the activity within the government, the military, and all other aspects of Soviet life, even to the highest echelons of power within the Kremlin itself.

During Malenkov's term in office, Krushchev quietly rallied the hard liners who were opposed to the premier's relaxation toward the West and the military, who had been deeply offended by cuts in military spending. He joined forces with Defense Minister Nikolai Bulganin and during a session of the Supreme Soviet in 1955, Malenkov's enemies, led by Krushchev, reversed this policy and forced him to resign as premier, and take the position of Deputy Premier. Bulganin became premier, and Krushchev took over as First Secretary of the Soviet Communist Party, the real seat of power. In March of 1958 Krushchev also took the title of premier and Bulganin was retired.

Krushchev was the leader of the Soviet Union for eight years, until October, 1964, when he was deposed and accused of 'errors,' including fomenting the Cuban missile crisis which caused embarrassment to the Soviet Union when Krushchev had to back down under the threat of nuclear war from the American president, John Kennedy. By the end of that year Krushchev no longer held political office and in 1966 he was dropped from the Central Committee.

The Fifth "King" — Brezhnev

Upon the political demise of Krushchev, Leonid Brezhnev became First Secretary of the Soviet Communist Party and Alexei Kosygin became premier, now relegated to a decidedly secondary position. Under Brezhnev's leadership, a new constitution was adopted by the

Supreme Soviet which dispelled any doubt about who ran the country — it was the Communist Party. Brezhnev was the leader of the Soviet Union for eighteen years until his death in 1982.

The Sixth "King" — Andropov

In a previous chapter we discussed Yuri Andropov's jockeying for position just prior to Brezhnev's death. Konstantin Chernenko had been the heir-apparent to Brezhnev, but with the KGB and Red Army behind him, no one dared challenge Andropov's power play.

Andropov lived for only fifteen months after being named General Secretary of the Soviet Communist Party. Confined to a sick bed most of that time, Andropov did not have the opportunity to consolidate his position nor to insure that his protege, Mikhail S. Gorbachev, would succeed him in office.

The Seventh "King" — Chernenko

Konstantin Chernenko's wait had not been in vain. Upon the death of Yuri Andropov, he was named General Secretary of the Soviet Communist Party. At seventy-two years of age, he was the oldest man ever selected to head the country. But he was also dying of emphysema and lived for only thirteen months.

The Eighth "King" — Gorbachev

On March 11, 1985, the Politburo elected Mikhail S. Gorbachev as General Secretary of the Soviet Communist Party and head of the nation.

Gorbachev is the eighth 'king' of the Soviet Union and the Revelation prophecy tells us that the antichrist will be the eighth in a line of leaders, or 'kings,' of a country. The same prophecy says that the seventh 'king' will continue in office for a 'short space.' Chernenko lived only thirteen months, certainly a 'short space.'

Mikhail S. Gorbachev meets this portion of the Revelation prophecy.

Has Anything Changed With Gorbachev?

Revelation 17:11 has this to say about the beast, "And the beast that was, and is not, even he is the eighth, and is of the seven, and goeth into perdition."

This tells us that the beast will be of the same ideology as the previous seven kings. He will be of the same mold as they were. The other leaders of the Soviet Union were all dedicated communists. To be this they had to disavow a belief in God. They had to pledge their loyalty to the aims of Marxist-Leninist doctrine which is the domination of the world by communism.

But Gorbachev has appealed to many in the West as a new type of Soviet leader. He is certainly more highly educated than any previous leader of that country, and more stylish in dress and manner. When Gorbachev and his attractive wife, Raisa, went to England, they were a sensation. Prime Minister Margaret Thatcher said, "I think we can do business with him."

But is he really any different than those who led the Soviet Union before? Are his aims any different than the aims of previous leaders were? According to Mikhail Tspkin, a specialist in Soviet studies at the Heritage Foundation in Washington and himself an emigre from the Soviet Union, he is not.

Tspkin said, "Gorbachev at home is pursuing a neo-Stalinist policy, which substitutes repression and mass mobilization for genuine economic reform. Gorbachev comes from the old mold. Far from being a reformer, he relies on traditional policies. There is no visible change in the Soviet regime's repressiveness, inefficiency, militarism or aggressiveness." [1]

Brother Andrew reports in "Open Doors News Brief," [2] that since Gorbachev had come to power, the arrest of Christians and dissidents have continued as before, but with a new twist. Just as these people are to be released after serving their prison sentences, they are resentenced for another five years.

Gorbachev is certainly of the same mold as his predecessors, but with one difference. If Gorbachev is the antichrist, then I do not believe he is truly an atheist. This may sound like a strange thing to say, but follow my reasoning and hear from Gorbachev's own lips a most interesting statement.

Mikhail S. Gorbachev, during an interview with Western reporters, said: "Surely God on high has not refused to give us enough wisdom to find ways to bring an improvement in relations between the two greatest nations on earth, nations on whom depends the very destiny of civilization."

Does this sound like a man who does not believe that God exists? When *PRAVDA* printed his statements, they deleted his reference to God on high, but those were his exact words.

Satan is not an atheist. He can't be, for he was created by God as the angel Lucifer — the most beautiful and intelligent of all the angels. God had given him a very special high place in heaven. But Lucifer rebelled against God, and convinced a third of the angels of heaven to join him in the rebellion. He was defeated, of course, for no one can rebel against God and not be defeated. He and the angels who had joined with him were cast out of heaven. Certainly Satan knows without a doubt that God exists — he even recognized Jesus and tried to tempt the Son of God into worshiping him. Satan cannot possibly be an atheist.

Would not, then, Satan's agent in the world — the antichrist — also know that God truly exists? Even the demons knew Jesus when He confronted them. The antichrist must certainly know what he is fighting against on earth, for his mission is to destroy Christianity and trick the world into worshiping him — and his master, Satan. It follows that the antichrist cannot be an atheist.

The Score — Gorbachev and the Antichrist Prophecy

Before we continue on with the vision of the end times John was given on the Isle of Patmos, let us look back and see how our candidate has fared with regard to the specifics of the antichrist prophecy.

1. THE NUMBER OF HIS NAME. We have seen that Gorbachev's name is a function of the number 666 when we use the values for the letters in both the Cyrillic and Hebrew alphabets after the name is transliterated into these languages. When we use the Greek transliteration, we find it is a function of 888 and 111, which are theomatic

designations for Jesus Christ. His name is also a function of 46, the 'number of man' which we found to be a hidden clue.

2. HIS SUDDEN APPEARANCE. He arose abruptly upon the world scene just as John describes the beast rising from the sea. We have seen that this is "Satan's sea" — the Soviet Union — which had a population of 276 million, Satan's theomatic number.

3. SEVEN HEADS. His seven heads are the seven Warsaw Pact nations.

4. THE NAME OF BLASPHEMY. The name written on each of his heads is communism — a name that is clearly blasphemous toward God.

5. TEN HORNS. His ten horns are the nations which the Soviet Union has devoured.

6. TEN CROWNS. Gorbachev wears the crowns of these ten nations.

7. BEAR'S FEET. His feet are those of a bear, the symbol of Russia.

8. LIKE A LEOPARD. He is the most highly educated man ever to head the Soviet Union, and he has the cunning of a leopard.

9. MOUTH OF A LION. When Gorbachev speaks, the world listens — as when a lion roars.

10. HIS POWER. The dragon, Satan, has given him his power, his seat, and great authority.

11. THE EIGHTH KING. We have seen that Gorbachev is the eighth leader, or 'king,' of the Soviet Union. He is of the same ideology as his predecessors.

12. TEN KINGS. The ten members of the Politburo elected him General Secretary of the Soviet Communist Party. These are kings without kingdoms as yet, who give their power and strength to Gorbachev. They serve at his discretion.

13. SATAN'S SEAT. We have seen that the Soviet Union is truly Satan's seat of power in the world today. Not only do theomatic clues of Satan's number appear as the values of Russian words, but no nation in history has treated its own citizens in the manner in which the Soviet Union has, disposing of unwanted people by the millions through execution or imprisonment in slave labor camps.

14. SATAN'S GOAL. We have seen that Satan's goal and the Soviet Union's goal are one in the same — world domination. The Soviet armed forces are the most powerful in history, and they are ideally suited for the antichrist to launch his campaign of conquest of the earth.

Prophecy Unfulfilled as Yet

15. THE DEADLY WOUND. The deadly wound to one of the beast's heads has not yet happened. Since the heads are the Warsaw Pact nations, one of these may possibly revolt, causing a 'wound' which would appear deadly to Gorbachev's political future.

16. THE DEADLY WOUND HEALED. This also is for the future. The revolt will be crushed, possibly by the use of nuclear weapons, and the world will be amazed at this. The false prophet will then appear on the scene.

Mikhail S. Gorbachev has fulfilled all of Revelation prophecy concerning the antichrst that is possible up to this point. Only the deadly wound and its healing, and the appearance of the false prophet, remain to be fulfilled before the antichrist begins his conquest and domination of the world.

Never before in history has any man fit the antichrist prophecy so exactly. Later in the book we will examine the statistical probability of his doing this and calculate the odds for and against Gorbachev being truly the antichrist.

6

The False Prophet
and the Mark of the Beast

*Insanity is a perfectly rational adjustment to an insane world.
(R.D. Laing)*

*Count it the greatest sin to prefer life to honor, and for the sake of
living to lose what makes life worth having. (Decimus Junius
Juvenal)*

Revelation 13:11 tells us about another beast which will arise in the
end times. He will work with the antichrist to establish Satan's will on
the earth, "And I beheld another beast coming up out of the earth: and
he had two horns like a lamb, and he spake as a dragon."

This is the false prophet. Satan is a master counterfeiter. Whatever
represents the true God, Satan will attempt to counterfeit by
producing a facsimile, something which appears very much like the
original but which is intrinsically evil. Satan's counterfeits bring
destruction to whatever they touch.

So it will be with the false prophet. It is Satan's intent to have the
world worship him in place of God, the Father. By raising up the
antichrist, he is counterfeiting the true Christ, the Son of God. Now, by
bringing forth the false prophet, Satan will attempt to counterfeit the
Holy Spirit of God, the third member of his evil trinity.

John tells us more about the false prophet in Revelation 13:12,
"And he exerciseth all the power of the first beast before him, and
causeth the earth and them that dwell therein to worship the first beast,
whose deadly wound was healed."

We see that the false prophet will be imbued with all the satanic
power the antichrist has been given. The two horns mean strength and

authority, which is from the Old Testament meanings of the word. The false prophet will probably be the leader of the worldwide false religion which in the end times will take the place of worship of the true God.

Many will be deceived by this false religion and will worship the beast and his master, Satan. Jesus warned of this in Matthew 24:24, "For there shall arise false Christs, and false prophets, and shall shew great signs and wonders; insomuch that, if it were possible, they shall deceive the very elect."

The false prophet will be able to perform what will appear to many to be great miracles, and signs and great wonders and much of the population of the earth will be completely taken in by these. John speaks of this in Revelation 13:13, "And he [the False Prophet] doeth great wonders, so that he maketh fire come down from heaven on the earth in the sight of men."

I believe there is a possibility that some of the wonders John speaks of will be the products of twentieth-century technology. In the time when John received his vision, not even gunpowder was known to the western world or the Middle East. Wars were fought with swords and spears and slings. It was in hand-to-hand combat that armies struggled. But in today's sophisticated arsenal of warfare, the trajectory of a ballistic missile takes it far above the earth — into heaven, so to speak — before it arches down to rain its fire upon the earth.

Could this passage in Revelation actually be describing a nuclear missile? If we think about how someone in the first century might depict such a weapon, John's description seems most apt indeed. Fire coming down from heaven would certainly have been a miracle in John's day, but we are not strangers to such a concept in today's world — held hostage, as we are, by threat of a nuclear holocaust.

Even in non-nuclear terms, the helicopter gunships used by American forces in Vietnam and the Soviets in Afghanistan "rain fire from the heavens." Napalm bombs do the same. If many of our modern technological achievements could have been shown to those in John's day, they could well have been described as miracles.

The Apostle John continues to talk about this false prophet, "And deceiveth them that dwell on earth by means of these miracles which he had the power to do in the sight of the beast; saying to them that dwell on the earth, that they should make an image to the beast, which had the wound by the sword and did live" (Rev. 13:14).

In the Soviet Union and other communist-controlled countries we see innumerable huge pictures of Lenin and communist leaders, some of them several stories tall, displayed prominently. Smaller photographs are found elsewhere — in homes, offices, stores and public buildings. Communism keeps the images of its heroes in front of the people constantly. In Red China, Mao's picture was displayed everywhere and almost all Chinese carried his "Little Red Book" of sayings.

Revelation 13:15 tells something else that the false prophet has the power to do, "And he had power to give life unto the image of the beast, that the image of the beast should both speak, and cause that as many as would not worship the image of the beast should be killed."

Could this be describing television broadcasts by the antichrist? It will certainly be broadcast by satellite to all parts of the world when he has conquered the earth and taken control of it. This would have indeed been called a miracle in John's day. Perhaps watching a daily broadcast by the antichrist will be mandatory for the entire world, and the penalty for ignoring his messages — death.

Worship of the antichrist may not be difficult to achieve in the end times. In every communist country today Lenin is revered with almost a religious adoration. Joseph Stalin fostered a personality cult where he was considered a personification of 'Father Russia.' The blind, fanatic worship of Adolf Hitler convinced millions of Germans that they could achieve the impossible and conquer the world. Prior to the end of World War II the Japanese considered their emperor a god.

Satan's insatiable desire to be worshiped as God will be manifested in this false religion and he will require adoration of him and the antichrist by all those living on the earth. Those who refuse will be killed, just as those who opposed Lenin, Stalin and Hitler were killed and those in ancient Rome who refused to worship the Emperor were either beheaded or fed to the lions.

The Mark of the Beast

To assure this unquestioned devotion, something else will be required and John tells us about it in Revelation 13:16, 17: "And he causeth all, both small and great, rich and poor, free or bond, to receive a mark in the right hand, or in their foreheads: And that no man might buy or sell, save he had the mark, or the name of the beast, or the number of his name."

There has been intense speculation about what this passage will mean in the end times, after the antichrist has taken control of the world. It appears that there will be three separate things or marks which will qualify a man to buy or sell. The first is called the 'Mark of the Beast.' If indeed the antichrist is the leader of the Soviet Union, then the mark may well be the Red Star — the universal communist symbol. This may be a simple tattoo of the communist Red Star.

A second possibility concerns what is meant by the 'name of the beast.' I do not think it will be the name of a specific man. The name referred to here might be the same as the name of blasphemy which appears on the heads of the beast. This mark again might be a simple tattoo indicating that the bearer is a member of the Communist Party, and loyal to the antichrist.

The third may be more complicated — the number of his name. I do not believe that this means simply the number 666. With the recent advancements in computer chip technology, especially in the miniaturization of them, it is now possible to make them microscopic enough to be injected beneath the skin. These chips could carry all the information about a person necessary to monitor his every movement and control all aspects of his life. The chip could be used to replace money, by electronically transferring funds. This technology exists now, including the software.

Although the microchip could possibly be the ultimate in the antichrist's control of people's lives, this would take considerable time to implement and the cost would be enormous. A much simpler form would be to use the series of bars utilized in the Universal Products Code already in place in most supermarkets. This code could be tattooed, possibly with a dye visible only under ultraviolet light, on either the hand or forehead. Scanners such as those in use in stores today could read the code and relay the information to central computers for processing or fund transfers.

Portable, hand-held scanner wands could be used by police and security officers for spot identification and conformance to the antichrist's rules.

Those who refuse to accept the mark of the beast or any of the other marks of identification would apparently be unable to buy even the necessities of life. If not executed by the antichrist's secret police, they and their families would eventually starve to death. But to accept this mark would be condemning oneself to an eternity of torment, for we are told in Revelation 14:9-10, "And the third angel followed them, saying with a loud voice, If any man worship the beast and his image, and receive his mark in his forehead, or in his hand, the same shall drink of the wine of the wrath of God, which is poured out without mixture into the cup of his indignation: he shall be tormented with fire and brimstone in the presence of the holy angels and in the presence of the Lamb."

This needs no clarification. The full and undiluted wrath of God will fall on anyone who worships the antichrist or Satan, or receives the mark in his hand or in his forehead. And they will be eternally tormented.

That this punishment will last forever is revealed in the next passage, "And the smoke of their torment ascendeth up for ever and ever: and they have no rest day or night, who worship the beast and his image, and whosoever receiveth the mark of his name" (Rev. 14:11).

Rationalization —the Self-Told Lie

You may be convinced that you will be able to resist the secret policemen who will tell you that if you refuse to have your hand tattooed you will be executed. You will know they'll do it because some members of your church will have already disappeared and you will be certain that they have died.

The police will tell you they will be back in a few days, that you had better make up your mind to conform. Then they will go away. Every day you will expect them to return, but they won't. In the meantime, you won't be able to buy any food and the pantry will be bare. What will you do when the food is completely gone?

I believe many people will face this situation and do exactly what the Hebrews did in the wilderness — they will rationalize and compromise.

After three hundred years of Egyptian slavery, God intervened and set the Hebrews free. Moses and Aaron stood firmly before Pharaoh and demanded the release of God's people. When Pharaoh refused, God struck the land with horrible plagues.

The final plague, and the one which convinced Pharaoh to free the Hebrews, took place on the first Passover. The death angels had slain all the firstborn of the land of Egypt, including Pharaoh's son, while the Hebrews were safe within their homes which had been marked by the lamb's blood above their doorways.

The Hebrews had been allowed to leave. They had seen God part the waters of the Red Sea and they had passed safely out of Egypt, while Pharaoh's army had been swallowed up by the water.

God had fed them with manna each morning. He had led them himself as a pillar of fire by night and a pillar of cloud by day. They had witnessed God's presence and care each day.

But when Moses was away from them for forty days and nights on the mountain — receiving God's laws — they became restless and fearful.

They said to Aaron, "Make us gods, which shall go before us, for as for this Moses, the man that brought us up out of the land of Egypt, we wot not what is become of him" (Exod. 32:1).

Aaron did as they asked. He melted down their golden earrings and cast a golden calf for them. Then the people bowed down to this idol and worshiped it, saying, "...these be the gods, O Israel, which brought thee up out of the land of Egypt" (Exod. 32:4).

Can you imagine this? After they had witnessed, *first-hand*, the power and the might of God, had seen His miracles on a daily basis, after he had freed them, fed them, led them personally through the wilderness, after they had passed safely through the parted waters of the Red Sea — they had Aaron make them an inert, dumb idol out of their golden earrings — and they worshipped it!

These people had seen, as no people before them had, the absolute power of God. Yet within a few weeks they had abandoned their faith and bowed down to a lifeless idol. They had rationalized their situation — and had told themselves a lie — that God no longer cared about them or their future. Or worse still, that God really did not exist. They thought Moses had died on the mountain and had left them leaderless.

Imagine this scenario. Your pantry has now been bare for weeks. There has been nothing to eat. You have refused to accept the tattoo on your hand. You can't talk with any other Christians, because they are either dead or have disappeared. Your children are starving. You hear them crying, not understanding why you don't feed them.

Your former friends, the people next door, have accepted the tattoo. Their children are fat and healthy. By now your children have lost so much weight that their ribs are beginning to show through their skin. You remember seeing children in Ethiopia who looked like this. You never dreamed your own children would have to suffer starvation. They are getting weaker day by day. They really do not cry now, it is more of a whimper. They don't understand why you won't give them anything to eat. All they know is that terrible gnawing in their empty stomachs and you won't do anything about it.

You think that for yourself, you could stand it. But the children...! Why does it have to be the children?

It is then that you begin to rationalize. After all, it's just a mere tattoo on the hand. That can't be the same as actually worshiping the image of the antichrist. Surely God will understand if I submit to having that little, inconsequential tattoo stamped on my hand. God loves my children. He wouldn't want them to starve. He would understand. Why, I bet He would *even approve of it* to save my children's lives. After all, *it's just an invisible tattoo*! It can't possibly hurt anything!

You tell yourself that God would never condemn you to eternal damnation for saving your own children.

Isn't that what the serpent told Eve?

"Surely you will not die!"

The Big Lie

Many people will believe the same big lie that Satan whispered into Eve's ear in the Garden of Eden. God has told us in no uncertain terms that to accept the mark of the beast means eternal torment and damnation. But Satan whispers the same lie in our ears: "Surely you will not die!"

Who will you believe under these circumstances, God or Satan?

7

Where Are We in Time?

Pygmies placed on the shoulders of giants see more than the giants themselves. (Lucan)

My interest is in the future because I am going to spend the rest of my life there. (Charles F. Kettering)

In this chapter we will examine the prophecy dealing with the last days. From this, it should be perfectly clear that now is the *exact time* for the antichrist to appear.

Even those who do not take biblical prophecy seriously agree that we are indeed living in perilous times. They admit that the awesome specter of nuclear annihilation casts chilling shadows on man's prospects for survival. In a recent survey made in this country, over sixty percent of the people interviewed expressed grave doubts about mankind's ability to survive another hundred years.

Many psychologists have reported that the irrational behavior of many of today's teenagers is a reflection of their doubt concerning whether they have any future to look forward to in this nuclear age. Suicide among teenagers now ranks as the second highest cause of death, surpassed only by the number of teens killed in automobile accidents. Even primary school children indicated that many of their worries are centered around the threat of nuclear war. This fear is certainly a reflection of what they are hearing at home, but the very fact that such young children are concerned about their lives is indicative of the widespread fear of this generation about the future.

The End-Times Prophecy

Jesus told His disciples, "For many shall come in my name, saying, I am Christ: and shall deceive many. And ye shall hear of wars and rumors of wars: see that ye be not troubled: for all these things must come to pass, but the end is not yet. For nation shall rise against nation, and kingdom against kingdom: and there shall be famines, and pestilences, and earthquakes, in divers places. All these are the beginning of sorrows" (Matt. 24:5-8).

These words from Jesus give us the signs of what He calls 'the beginning of sorrows,' which is the prelude to the coming of the antichrist and the Great Tribulation which He tells His disciples about in a later verse from the Scriptures.

Let us look closely at these signs before we move on into additional end-times prophecy.

False Religions

It has been almost 2,000 years since Jesus gave the Great Commission to His disciples. Even so, only 21 percent of the world's population claim to be Christians. Christianity does, however, represent the single largest segment of the world's religions, but I cannot help but wonder just how pleased Jesus is with the success of His missionaries. Islam, founded about six hundred years later, is the second largest world religion with 12 percent of the people of the earth adhering to its teachings.

Mohammed was certainly a false Christ, for he claimed to have been sent by God to complete the work Jesus had left undone. But I believe the warning about false Christs also applies to the plethora of cults which have risen recently, many of them originating from Eastern mystical religions. These have invaded the West and have attracted millions of followers.

In the United States alone it is estimated that over ten million people have abandoned their traditional faith and have become involved with these cults, some of which openly worship Satan. In many cities young followers of the Hare Krishna movement are much in evidence, selling flowers and trinkets to support this cult. The 'Moonies' are led by a Korean, Dr. Moon, who claims to be the reincarnate Christ.

Antelope, Oregon, was recently the site of a community founded by an Indian guru, Bhagwan Shree Rajneesh, who left behind his expensive automobiles when he fled the country to avoid legal prosecution for fraud. The tragic suicide of the followers of Jim Jones in Guyana points out just how seriously many take the words and teachings of these self-appointed messiahs.

The ultimate false Christ will be the true antichrist. Compared with other religious charlatans, the success he will have in mass deception will be without equal. In fact, the vast majority of the world's population will be completely taken in by him, even to the point of worshiping him as God. He will indeed be the ultimate false Christ.

The antichrist will certainly be fully supported by those already involved in Satan worship. This cult has grown dramatically in recent years and has infected many segments of today's society. The New Age movement may also be involved in proclaiming the authority of the antichrist. This rapidly growing movement has already attracted many well-known personalities such as Shirley MacLaine. It is quite possible that Satan will use the New Age Channelers to proclaim Mikhail S. Gorbachev as the only man capable of solving the world's problems and hailing him as the New Age "savior," which is exactly how the antichrist will present himself to the world in the last days.

Wars and Rumors of Wars

The entire history of mankind has been bloody. War has been very much a part of man's life since the first wandering tribe fought with another tribe with clubs and stones to drive them away from the best foraging area for food.

No nation has ever existed which has not, at one time or another, been at war with a neighbor or suffered an internal conflict. The Bible narrates countless episodes of Israel's battles against other tribes and people.

But never has the world seen such a bloody century as this one. More people have been killed by war in the twentieth century than in all the rest of recorded history. At this writing more than forty wars are being waged. One out of every four nations in the world is involved in some degree of conflict, either with another nation or in an internal rebellion.

Actually, World War II never ceased. It simply broke up into a series of smaller, but just as deadly, regional conflicts. Some are still raging. The nation of Israel, born out of the holocaust of Hitler's death camps, has almost continually had to defend her right to exist against the Arab countries which surround her.

The prime factor which has motivated this continual warfare in the world since 1945 has been the export of communist revolution into the countries of the underdeveloped Third World. Since the end of official hostilities with Germany and Japan, wars have raged in Europe, Africa, Asia and South America. Of the populated continents, only North America and Australia have thus far escaped this post-war bloodbath.

The major wars which have occurred since 1945 are listed in Exhibit III by geographic areas.

EXHIBIT III

MAJOR WARS SINCE 1945

ASIA

China, Civil War
Indonesia, Independence
Indochina, First War
Philippines, Huk Revolt
Burma, Karen Revolt
Malaya, Communist Insurgency
Korea, Korean Conflict
Tibet, Revolt Against China
Indochina, Second War
India-China, Border War
Malaysia, Indonesian Dispute
India-Pakistan, War
China-USSR, Border Conflict
India-Pakistan, Second War
Philippines, Muslim Revolt
East Timor, Indonesian Invasion

Kampuchea, Vietnamese Invasion
Vietnam, Vietnamese War
Cambodia, Vietnamese Invasion

EUROPE

Greece, Communist Revolt
East Germany, Soviet Invasion
Poland, Soviet Intervention
Hungary, Soviet Intervention
Czechoslovakia, Soviet Intervention
Northern Ireland, IRA Rebellion

LATIN AMERICA

Cuba, Revolution
Bay of Pigs, Failed Invasion
San Domingo, U.S. Intervention
Guatemala, Civil War
Nicaragua, Revolution
El Salvador, Civil War
Falkland Islands, Argentine Invasion
Grenada, U.S. Intervention
Nicaragua, Counter-Revolution

AFRICA

Madagascar, Malagasy Revolt
Kenya, Mau-Mau War
Tunisia, War of Independence
Morocco, War of Independence
Algeria, War of Independence
Suez, War
Congo, Civil War
Ethiopia, Eritrean Revolt
Angola, War of Independence
Guinea, War of Independence
Mozambique, War of Independence

Rhodesia, Zimbabwean Revolt
Nigeria, Civil War
Angola, Civil War
Namibia, War of Independence
Ogaden, War
Sahel, War
Tanzania, Invasion of Uganda

MIDDLE EAST

Israel, Arab War
Cyprus, Civil Unrest
Sinai, Egypt-Israeli War
Lebanon, Israeli Invasion
Yemen, Civil War
Aden, War of Independence
Israel, Six Day War
Israel, Yom Kippur War
Cyprus, Turkish Invasion
Lebanon, Civil War
Afghanistan, Soviet Invasion
Iran-Iraq, War
South Yemen, Civil War

The Undeclared War

In addition to 'official' wars, there is an ongoing conflict which knows neither boundary nor combatant. This is the horror of international terrorism which is sweeping the earth. The hijacking of planes and ships has placed the innocent traveler in direct jeopardy today.

Bombs have exploded on streets, in stores, train stations, airline terminals, anywhere crowds may be found — killing hundreds each year, primarily helpless women and children. The American military overseas have been a prime target, with barracks and nightclubs frequented by U.S. servicemen especially vulnerable. A number of

American embassy personnel have been assassinated and U.S. Embassies have been damaged by terrorist bombs.

I believe this will get worse, despite American retaliation against Khadafy's home base in Libya, with terrorist attacks eventually reaching even to American cities. The madmen of Khadafy, the fanatic Islamic Jihad, and the PLO have sworn to bring this senseless and savage war of terror to American soil, and I believe they will.

Never before in history has war been brought home to as many in the world as it has been in this century. And the 'rumors of war,' meaning the threat of conflict, is ever-present in the minds of the vast majority of the world's population, with the prospect of global nuclear annihilation holding the earth captive to fear.

The prophecy of Jesus concerning wars and rumors of war certainly applies to the world right now. Look at the front page of the newspaper and you will see the fulfilling of that prophecy of the end times. We are living in the "time of sorrows," the prelude to the Great Tribulation. It has happened to us — in our generation.

Famine

The population of the world now exceeds five billion. Unfortunately, most population growth is occurring in parts of the world which cannot raise sufficient food for the people in those regions. Babies are being born today in many parts of the world with the odds stacked against their survival, even through the first year of their lives. There has always been famine in world history, but never before have so many people faced the prospect of starvation on such an enormous scale.

Sixty percent of the world (three billion people) go hungry every day and suffer from malnutrition to some degree. Half of the children born today will go through life without even once having the experience of a full stomach.

It is only when the television cameras bring the stark reality of famine to our eyes, such as occurred recently in Ethiopia, that we in America recognize what the majority of the world faces on a continual basis. It is estimated that today there are as many as five

million people who die from starvation each year. This means that *one person starves to death somewhere in the world every six seconds!*
If that is not the fulfillment of Jesus' prophecy of great famine, I don't know what would be!

Pestilence

Worldwide epidemics have been held somewhat in check by modern antibiotics, but recent events are pointing to several situations which may mean serious and widespread disease on the immediate horizon for which medical science has no cure. The number of Americans who have been exposed to the virus which causes AIDS is estimated to be over one million, and is expected to at least double each year.

Venereal diseases, once believed to be under control, have increased at alarming rates. New strains of syphilis and gonorrhea are proving highly resistant to the antibiotics which at one time kept them in check. Herpes and other relatively unknown types of venereal diseases are increasing drastically, with little success in treating them.

Each winter a new influenza outbreak strikes the world. Although vaccines can be prepared which prevent or mitigate these potentially dangerous outbreaks, it is quite possible that some new and particularly virulent strain may appear so suddenly that there will be no time to develop or produce a vaccine against it. A worldwide epidemic similar to or worse than the 1918 influenza epidemic could very possibly occur, resulting in tens of millions of deaths in a short period of time.

The Western world has not been recently exposed to the ravages of widespread and deadly epidemics, but the Third World countries know them all too well. Malnutrition lowers body resistance and poor sanitation spreads disease quickly. Lack of adequate medical facilities leaves the poor of the underdeveloped countries without treatment. But the affluence of the West is no guarantee against epidemics. New diseases, such as AIDS, could produce just such a deadly plague, especially now that it has spread to the heterosexual community. This epidemic could possibly kill more people than any outbreak of disease since the great plagues of the Middle Ages.

Earthquakes

Each year there are an estimated 100,000 earthquakes in the world. Fortunately, most of these are too slight even to be measured by any but the most sensitive seismic equipment, and the majority of these do no harm. But recently there has been a drastic increase in the number of severe earthquakes and these have occurred near population centers, causing many deaths and much property damage.

I believe the data on earthquakes given below will surprise many people:

Earthquakes [1]	Deaths	Periods
From 500 AD to 1900AD	2,315,000	1400 Years
In this century through 1985	1,522,000	85 Years

From 500 to 1900 AD an average of 165,000 deaths occurred per century from earthquakes. But in only eighty-five years of this century, there have been 1,522,000 deaths. This is an increase of over 900 percent.

This, too, is a fulfillment of Jesus' prophecy concerning the events of the end times. We will have more to say concerning earthquakes in a later chapter where we deal with the fate of the United States in the end times.

There have been a series of moderate earthquakes recently in California, but as one seismologist put it, "They have been just fender benders compared to the expected Big One." The one which struck at 7:42 in the morning of October 1, 1987, killed eight people, destroyed twenty-six buildings, damaged dozens of others, and caused more than 213 million dollars in property losses.

But these figures are nothing compared to the 'Big One' expected in the future. This quake was along a small fault, the Whittier, which runs parallel to the San Andreas fault. It measured 5.8 on the Richter scale. The 'Big One' along the San Andreas fault could easily reach a Richter force of 8 or more, which means the pending disaster would pack a punch more than 900 times that of the October 1, 1987, quake. It is not a case of if, say seismologists, only of when and how big.

Although comparative data is not available for deaths due to storms, floods and tidal waves, it is interesting to look at these figures since the beginning of this century.

	Deaths
Storms: Hurricanes, Typhoons, etc. Since 1900	475,000
Floods and Tidal Waves, Deaths Since 1900	4,065,000

Over six million people have been killed so far in this century by earthquakes, storms and floods. Prospects are that things will get worse, not better. The 1906 earthquake, which destroyed San Francisco, killed only 503 people. It is estimated that an earthquake of the same magnitude today would kill between 200,000 and 500,000 people.

Moral Degeneration

The Apostle Peter spoke of how low the morality of the people in the end times would sink. In Second Peter 2:10-14, he tells us, "But chiefly them that walk after the flesh in the lust of uncleanness, and despise government. Presumptuous are they, self-willed, they are not afraid to speak evil of dignities. Having eyes full of adultery, and that cannot cease from sin; beguiling unstable souls: an heart they have exercised with covetous practices; cursed children...."

The sexual revolution has so conditioned society that most people today are shock-proof. Promiscuity is rampant among teenagers. With many adults, adultery has become an accepted norm. Marriage is old-fashioned, out-of-date, and divorce is often taken as lightly as buying a new suit of clothes.

The Apostle Paul could peer down the long corridor of time and describe to Timothy what conditions would be like in the end times. In Second Timothy 3:1-4, he wrote, "This know also, that in the last days perilous times shall come. For men shall be lovers of their own selves, covetous, boasters, proud, blasphemers, disobedient to parents, unthankful, unholy. Without natural affection, trucebreakers, false accusers, incontinent, fierce, dispersers of those that are good,

Traitors, heady, highminded, lovers of pleasure more than lovers of God."

Paul was looking right at our society of today when he wrote this. He could have just as well been speaking of Sodom and Gomorrah, for we have become very much like those wicked cities which the Lord saw fit to completely destroy.

Our society today has accepted homosexuality just as readily as it had accepted many other immoral acts. What God, in His Word, has called an 'abomination,' we refer to as 'an alternative life style.' Perhaps our terminology has changed, but God's has not; to God homosexuality is still an abomination.

Homosexuals are called the 'Gay Community.' From what I have observed of them, homosexuals are anything but happy and light-hearted (the true definition of "gay"). Homosexuality and lesbianism are unnatural acts and are sins against, not only one's own body — but against God. Homosexual acts are an abomination to Him.

The biblical prophecy concerning the immorality which would take over our society in the end times is already here. And we will have to answer to God for every part of it when the final judgment comes upon our country.

High Society

One of the cruelest tricks Satan has played upon the world today is the lure of 'getting high.' Unable to inspire the same effect which the Christian gets from the daily walk with the Lord, Satan has flooded our society with a blatant lie — the 'high' produced by narcotics.

Unable — or unwilling — to cope with the normal pressures of life, millions of young people have turned to the temporary escape which narcotics initially give, only to find themselves trapped in the steel cage of addiction which is a living hell. I am certain that the vast majority of people believe they will not become drug addicts, that they will be able to stop anytime they desire. They mean to try it only once or twice to please their peers. But when Satan gets his hook into them, he doesn't let go easily.

Many are addicts before they realize it, with an ever-increasing demand, an increasingly more expensive habit to satisfy. When an addict cannot afford to supply his requirement from personal funds, he must obtain the money from somewhere else. Thousands of teen-age girls are forced into prostitution each year because of their drug habits. Young boys resort to burglary, theft, and prostitution. Police departments have estimated that well over half of the crime in the country today is drug-related. Addicts will kill, if necessary, to get money for a fix.

Illegal drugs have become a big business in our society. A recent government study estimates that organized crime does 200 billion dollars in illegal narcotics business each year. To get an idea of just how large a sum that is, the federal budget deficit in 1984 was less, some 175 billion dollars.

In that same year, the total federal budget was 841 billion dollars. The business which organized crime does in narcotics amounted to 24 percent of that year's *total federal spending.* With such astronomical sums as this at stake, there are unlimited funds available to bribe officials in order to protect this business.

Each year Satan's arm seems to reach younger and younger children, even students in primary schools today. There is absolutely no place in America where drugs cannot be obtained, even within the prisons among inmates who are incarcerated on drug charges.

With borders as open as those of the United States are, it is impossible to stem the flow of narcotics into this country no matter how much additional money is spent, or how many border patrolmen are added. It would seem that the only way to stop the illegal narcotics business in the United States would be to take the profit out of it by making narcotics available to addicts legally by the government. But this is not likely to happen.

Cocaine has taken over as the major drug in use today, with the more powerful and cheaper form of it, known as 'crack,' taking over much of the narcotics business. This form is so powerful that many are 'hooked' after only one use.

It seems that drugs are with us to stay, and their use will increase each year. Satan has not just whispered this lie into the ears of our youths — he has shouted it, and they have responded. We are indeed well into the period which Jesus called the 'beginning of sorrows.'

Lawlessness

Biblical prophecy states that in the last days there will be a blatant disregard for law and order, eventually leading to a society of lawlessness. This has been very much in evidence in our cities for some time, and now crime is moving rapidly into the suburbs and rural areas. Families who but a few years ago could leave their doors unlocked now live behind bars on their windows and dead-bolt locks on their doors. Crime has reached epidemic proportions in some areas. Older Americans admit to being fearful for their safety, even when locked within their homes and apartments. It is no longer safe even to walk the streets after dark in many areas, and not safe even in broad daylight in others.

The following crime statistics speak for themselves, and these are from America — the land of the free:

- There is a murder every twenty-eight seconds. In 1984 there were 18,690 murders.
- There is a forcible rape every six seconds. A 50 percent increase since 1975.
- There is one robbery every second, day and night.
- There is one aggravated assault every 0.8 seconds. An increase of 395 percent since 1975.
- There are five burglaries every second. A 10 percent increase over 1975.
- There are twelve larcenies every second. A 10 percent increase over 1975.
- There are two car thefts every second.

Can anyone disagree that we are indeed living in a lawless society, just as the end-times prophecies predict?

Many people today have lost all hope. Our final statistic in this section proves this contention:

Every eighteen seconds an American commits suicide. There are 10,000 more victims of suicide each year in this country than victims of murder.

Science and Technology

John was not the only man who was given a glimpse of the end times. Five hundred years before, Daniel was given a vision in which he was told what these final days would be like: "But Daniel, keep this prophecy a secret; seal it up so that it will not be understood until the end times, when travel and education shall be vastly increased" (Dan. 12:4, TAB).

Daniel was told to seal up the book until the end times when people could understand it. We are that generation.

Certainly travel and education have vastly increased. Men have, in our generation, traveled not only to all parts of the earth, but to the moon and back.

We can board a plane in Los Angeles, circle over the Pacific Ocean as we take off, fly across the country and be over the Atlantic Ocean in five hours, landing at Boston. We are a generation of travelers, indeed.

Knowledge has increased at such a rate that man must use artificial methods, such as computers, to keep track of it. It has been estimated that fifty years ago, only 10 percent of our current knowledge was available. As a young engineering student, I thought my slide rule was high technology. Today slide rules are museum pieces. If someone would have told me then about the computers of today, I probably would not have believed them.

There is no doubt that this generation has fulfilled the prophecy given in Daniel about travel and education being greatly increased in the end times. But we have sometimes mistaken knowledge for wisdom, and that may prove to be a fatal mistake for many in these last few years of life on earth. People have ignored what a very wise man said about three thousand years ago: "The fear of the Lord is the beginning of wisdom: and the knowledge of the holy is understanding" (Prov. 9:10).

Modern technology has brought about the fulfillment of another end-times prophecy. Television and radio, with orbiting satellites able to beam programing to all parts of the globe, has fully allowed this part of Jesus' last-days events to be accomplished. "And this gospel of the kingdom shall be preached in all the world for a witness unto all nations; and then shall the end come" (Matt. 24:14).

There is not a nation in the world where the gospel has not been preached. Even when the government has forbidden evangelists to enter a country, radio broadcasts have reached the people. Cheap transistor radios have brought even primitive villages into direct contact with the outside world, and have brought the gospel messages to the most remote jungle outposts. The gospel *has* been preached to all nations. Jesus did not say that these nations had to *receive* it, only that it had to be preached. There is nothing in this prophecy yet to be fulfilled which would delay the end-times events from happening.

The Rebirth of Israel

Just a short time before Jesus was crucified, He looked upon the city of Jerusalem and wept. We are given His words: "O Jerusalem, Jerusalem, thou that killest the prophets, and stonest them which are sent unto thee, how often would I have gathered thy children together, even as a hen gathered her chickens under her wings, and ye would not! Behold, your house is left unto you desolate. For I say unto you, Ye shall not see me henceforth, till ye shall say, Blessed is he that cometh in the name of the Lord" (Matt. 23:37-39).

The Jews had rejected Him as their Messiah. Not all of them had, but the high priests and the religious leaders had been afraid of Him, afraid of the power He had over the masses of people. They conspired with the Roman authorities to have Him put to death. Jesus knew what was going to happen. In these verses He is telling the people of Jerusalem that they would not see Him again until the Second Coming, when He would return in power and glory and they could not possibly mistake Him for anything but the Messiah.

But Jerusalem and all of Palestine would be punished — literally destroyed — because they had not received Him when he came to them.

In Luke 21:20-22, this is foretold, "And when ye shall see Jerusalem compassed with armies, then know that the desolation thereof is nigh. Then let them that are in Judaea flee to the mountains; and let them that are in the midst of it depart out; and let not them that are in the countries enter thereinto. For these be the days of vengeance, that all things which are written may be fulfilled."

This is a prophecy from Jesus in which He states that Jerusalem would be destroyed and the Jews dispersed into the Gentile nations. About the great Temple which had been constructed by Herod and just recently been completed, He had this to say: "...Seest thou these great buildings? there shall not be left one stone upon another, that shall not be thrown down" (Mark 13:2).

This was said in 33 AD and in 70 AD the Roman army under Titus utterly destroyed Jerusalem and the great Temple. About one million Jews from the surrounding areas had fled into Jerusalem for safety, for the Romans were killing any Jews they found. Jesus had warned them to flee into the mountains, but they had fled instead to Jerusalem. After the destruction of the city, only about fifty thousand Jews survived to be sold into slavery or killed in the Roman sporting arenas. The rest had perished.

The words of one Roman officer have been recorded, "It looked as though no one had ever lived there. Not one stone was left upon another." These were almost the exact words Jesus had used, and the Jews were to remain scattered among the Gentile nations for almost 2,000 years.

The prophet Ezekiel lived and wrote at the same time as Daniel. He, too, had been given a vision of the end times. One of the events he saw was the return of the Jews to their homeland and this is described in Ezekiel 36:24, "For I will take you from among the heathen, and gather you out of all countries, and bring you into your own land."

This, of course, was realized in 1948 with the rebirth of the nation of Israel. Jesus had prophesied the same thing and has also given us another event with which to mark the appearance of the end times. Jesus said, "...and Jerusalem shall be trodden down of the Gentiles, until the times of the Gentiles be fulfilled" (Luke 21:24).

This has also occurred. In 1967 Israeli troops occupied all of Jerusalem, marking the lifting of the Gentile foot from the city.

Jesus gave us another clue to the final countdown in Luke 21:32, "Verily I say unto you, This generation shall not pass away, till all be fulfilled."

Which generation was Jesus speaking of here? He was speaking of the generation which will see these signs of the end times coming to pass. We are that generation. A generation is taken to mean forty years, and our current generation will not pass away until everything prophesied about the end of the world actually happens.

What About the Temple Being Rebuilt?

There are some people who hold the view that the Temple must be rebuilt in Jerusalem before the Lord returns. They take a passage from the book of Amos as their source. In the King James translation of the Bible we read, "In that day I will raise up the tabernacle of David that is fallen...." The word here is 'tabernacle' and this has been incorrectly translated. This was corrected in the Revised Standard Version, which agrees now with the Hebrew word. This reads as follows from Amos 9:11, "In that day I will raise up the booth of David that is fallen and repair its breaches, and raise up its ruins, and rebuild it as in the days of old" (RSV).

What is David's booth? To celebrate the Feast of Tabernacles, all the people went outside the walls of the city and lived in makeshift huts or tents. In David's case, being the king, he had a stone enclosure with freshly cut branches of trees for a roof.

A few years ago, a team of archaeologists from a university in Texas joined with a group of Israeli archaeologists in digging in the area where the old wall was located. They just happened to find the remains of — you guessed it! — David's booth, right where it should have been. The stones had fallen down and it was in ruins, but that's just the way the prophecy says it should be when it is found.

They raised it up again, repaired its breaches, and rebuilt it as in the days of old. This prophecy *has been fulfilled*. There is no reason to blow up the Mosque of Omar and rebuild the Temple. There is no end-times prophecy that says this has to happen. David's booth has been rebuilt with its original stones.

But Just Where Are We in Time?

Let's get to the heart of what this chapter is about — exactly where are we in time? Where do we stand in relation to the events which will occur in the very final years of this world? When will Jesus return?

To answer this, we must ask ourselves whether the evidence about Mikhail S. Gorbachev being the true antichrist is convincing. If he is indeed the antichrist, we can pinpoint exactly where we are in the timetable given in John's book of Revelation.

John saw the beast — the antichrist — several times in his vision. We have already discussed where he is seen rising out of the sea. But John saw him again, when the Lamb opened the seals of the book, which Daniel had also seen but which had remained hidden until the last days: "And I saw when the Lamb opened one of the seals, and I heard, as it were the noise of thunder, one of the four beasts saying, Come and see. And I saw, and behold a white horse: and he that sat on him had a bow; and a crown was given unto him: and he went forth conquering and to conquer."

John sees the antichrist upon a white horse — the symbol of a conqueror, when the Lamb opens the First Seal. The antichrist has a bow — a symbol of military might. He is given a crown — he is 'king' of a country. He rides forth conquering and to conquer.

Gorbachev has the bow in his hand, the most powerful military force in history. Gorbachev wears a crown; he is leader of the Soviet Union. Gorbachev has *not yet* ridden forth, conquering and to conquer — the world.

Where are we in time: If Gorbachev is truly the antichrist — then *the first seal of the book has already been opened by the Lamb!* THE FINAL COUNTDOWN HAS ALREADY STARTED.

Several years ago a team of archaeologists discovered an Egyptian calendar which had been buried for about 6,000 years. This calendar not only recorded the years past in history but far into the future. The ancient Egyptians used the solar year in reckoning time so that the years on this calendar correspond to our own.

The last year recorded on this ancient calendar is the equivalent to our year of 2001 AD.

Halfway around the world in Central America, another team of archaeologists unearthed another ancient calendar, a Mayan one estimated to be over 1,000 years old. The Mayans also used the solar year to reckon time and their year also corresponded to our own. This calendar projected years into the future as the Egyptian calendar did.

The last year recorded on this ancient Mayan calendar was the equivalent of our year 2001 AD.

The last event I want to share with you occurred in July, 1985, and what makes it even more unusual is the source from which it comes. At the end of 1985, the Sunday newspaper supplement, "Parade Magazine," printed a series of what they considered to be the strangest stories of the past year. Under the heading of 'Best International News,' they reported the following:

"Six Soviet cosmonauts said they witnessed the most awe-inspiring spectacle ever encountered in space — a band of glowing angels with wings as big as jumbo jets. According to *Weekly World News* [2], cosmonauts Vladimir Solevev, Oleg Atkov and Leonid Kizim said they first saw the celestial beings last July, during their 155th day aboard the orbiting Salyud 7 space station. 'What we saw', they said, 'were seven giant figures in the form of humans, but with wings and mistlike halos, as in the classic depiction of angels. Their faces were round with cherubic smiles.' Twelve days later, the figures returned and were seen by three other Soviet scientists, including woman cosmonaut Svetlana Savitskaya. 'They were smiling,' she said, 'as though they shared in a glorious secret.'"

I wonder what that secret was!

How Much Time Is Left?

Jesus told us, "But of that day and hour knoweth no man, no, not the angels of heaven, but my Father only" (Matt. 24:36).

He was speaking here of His return to earth as King of kings and Lord of lords, coming to do battle with the antichrist at the Battle of Armageddon.

But He also told us that we should be able to tell the *approximate* time of His coming from what was happening in the world. He gave us this information, "Now learn a parable of the fig tree; When his branch is yet tender, and putteth forth leaves, ye know that summer is nigh: So likewise ye, when ye shall see all these things, know that it is near, even at the doors. Verily I say unto you, This generation shall not pass, till all these things be fulfilled" (Matt. 24:32-34).

We have seen the fig tree, Israel, put forth her tender shoots. We have seen the Gentile foot removed from Jerusalem in the 1967 War. We have seen the events which Jesus has termed the Beginning of Sorrows come to pass, with increases in earthquakes, wars, rumors of wars, famine, new diseases, false messiahs, and the gospel preached to all the nations of the world.

And if Mikhail S. Gorbachev is truly the antichrist, then the first seal has already been opened and the final countdown has begun.

Jesus told us that the generation which observes these signs and events will not pass away until *everything* in the end-times prophecy has been accomplished, including His Second Coming. If we read this prophecy correctly, the generation He refers to begins with the Gentile foot being removed from Jerusalem. This happened in 1967. One full generation of forty years would bring us to the year 2007 AD. But remember, this is the *maximum* time we would have left to fulfill *all* of the prophecy, including the antichrist conquering the world, the Battle of Armageddon, and the Second Coming of Jesus Christ.

We were not told that the full time of this generation would be left, only that these events would occur *sometime during* that generation.

Using this timetable, sometime very soon we will be entering the period which Jesus has called the Great Tribulation. Before this, the antichrist will have embarked on his conquest of the world. And he will succeed in conquering it, for the prophecy tells us he will.

8

How Accurate
Has Biblical Prophecy Been?

*The whole of history is incomprehensible without the Christ.
(Ernest Renan)*

*The New Testament, and to a very large extent the Old, is the soul
of man. You cannot criticize it. It criticizes you. (John Jay
Chapman)*

The Bible consists of sixty-six individual books written over a
period of about 2,000 years. It is divided into two sections, the Old and
New Testaments. Among the many things these books contain are
prophecies made by men who claimed to be speaking for God.

There is but one way to judge a prophet. If his prophecy comes true,
then he is indeed a prophet. If his prophecies do not come about, he is a
fraud. We will look at a few of the most startling examples of biblical
prophecy and see for ourselves whether we should take biblical
prophecy seriously.

The author of the book of Amos tells us that we should indeed take
them seriously, for they really are prophets of God. "Surely the Lord
God will do nothing, but he revealeth his secret to his servants, the
prophets" (Amos 3:7).

Let us see for ourselves whether this is true, and God actually does
control the events of this world and tells of them in advance through
certain men.

Isaiah lived in about 700 BC. During his lifetime the great and
beautiful temple which Solomon had constructed was standing in
splendor and the city of Jerusalem was prospering. But Isaiah

prophesied that both would be destroyed and that the Hebrews would be taken captive by Babylon. This was written over a hundred years before this was to take place. This did indeed happen, but it is not the most startling of Isaiah's prophecies.

Isaiah wrote down the exact name of the man who would release the Hebrews after their Babylonian captivity — calling him by his name over 200 years before this man would be born. Look at what he said in Isaiah 44:26-28, "But what my prophets say, I do; when they say Jerusalem will be delivered and the cities of Judah lived in once again — it shall be done! When I speak to the rivers and say, Be dry! they shall be dry. When I say of Cyrus, He is my shepherd, he will certainly do as I say; and Jerusalem will be rebuilt and the Temple restored, for I have spoken it" (*TLB*).

When this was written, the city and the Temple were still standing and there was no threat of them being destroyed. But God, through Isaiah, is talking about them being restored, and at this time no one knew just who this man Cyrus would be.

God had more to say about Cyrus, "This is Jehovah's message to Cyrus, God's anointed, whom he has chosen to conquer many lands. God shall empower his right hand and he shall crush the strength of mighty kings. God shall open the gates of Babylon to him; the gates shall not be shut against him any more. I will go before you, Cyrus, and level the mountains and smash down the city gates of brass and iron bars. And I will give you treasures hidden in the darkness, secret riches; and you will know that I am doing this — I, the Lord, the God of Israel, the one who calls you by your name" (Isa. 45:1-3, *TLB*).

History has recorded the fulfillment of this prophecy. In 586 BC, more than a hundred years after Isaiah's prophecy, Nebuchadnezzar of Babylon destroyed Jerusalem and Solomon's temple. The Hebrews were taken captive back to Babylon. After seventy years, the Persian king, Cyrus, conquered Babylon and allowed the Hebrews to return home and to rebuild the city and the Temple.

Cyrus established the mighty and wealthy Persian empire which was to remain until another world conqueror, Alexander the Great, would defeat the Persians in 333 BC. This, incidentally, was also foretold in biblical prophecy, by Daniel (Dan. 8:21).

How was Isaiah able to predict these events accurately even down to the exact name of the Persian king? The only answer is that Isaiah was truly speaking for God, and that God does indeed control the fate and destiny of the world and its events.

The exact length of the Hebrew captivity by Babylon was prophesied by Jeremiah, who lived when they were first taken captive. "And this whole land shall be a desolation, and an astonishment; and these nations shall serve the king of Babylon seventy years" (Jer. 25:11).

Not only were the circumstances and exact names foretold by God's prophets, but they also predicted the term of the captivity in Babylon.

Daniel, who prophesied the overthrow of the Persians by the Greeks under Alexander, made one of the most amazing prophecies in the Bible. He gave the exact year in which the Messiah, the Christ, would appear in history. Daniel 9:25 tells us, "Know therefore and understand, that from the going forth of the commandment to restore and build Jerusalem unto the Messiah, the Prince shall be seven weeks, and threescore and two weeks: the street shall be built again, and the wall, even in troublous times."

The period of time was given in weeks of years, not unusual in biblical prophecy and perfectly understood by those who heard and read it. This period of time was to be sixty-nine weeks times seven, or 483 years.

We must pay attention to all parts of prophecy to get its true meaning. Cyrus had allowed the Hebrews to return to Judaea with permission to rebuild the city and the Temple, but he did not give permission to rebuild the walls. And in the early part of the sixth century BC there was peace, not troublous times.

It was not until about 450 BC when Nehemiah obtained permission from Artaxerxes to rebuild the walls of Jerusalem for protection against the Samaritans, that the prophetic conditions were met and the countdown began. When we count 483 years from this point we get the year 33 AD, when Jesus was crucified and arose from the dead to become totally and finally the long-awaited Messiah.

As amazing as Daniel's prophecy concerning the date of the coming of the Messiah, Jesus Christ, is it is but one of over 300 individual prophecies in the Old Testament concerning the Christ. All of these had to be fulfilled during the lifetime of one person.

In His last twenty-four hours, before He died on the cross, Jesus had to fulfill thirty-one prophecies, all written hundreds of years before and recorded in the Old Testament. If you are familiar with the last day, when Jesus was seized by the soldiers, tried before the Roman proconsul Pontius Pilate, and crucified — they will all be familiar to you. But remember that these are all from the Old Testament, written many years before the birth of Jesus.

Prophecy Fulfilled by Jesus in His Last Twenty-four Hours

1. He would be betrayed by a friend.   Psalms 55:12-14; 41:9
2. He would be sold for thirty pieces of silver.   Zechariah 11:2
3. The money would be used to buy a potter's field. Zechariah 11:13
4. He disciples would forsake Him.   Zechariah 13:7
5. He would be accused by false witnesses.   Psalms 35:11; 109:2
6. He would be beaten and spat upon.   Isaiah 50:4-6
7. He would remain silent before His accusers.   Isaiah 53:7
8. He would be wounded and bruised.   Isaiah 53:5, 6, 10
9. He would be nailed to a cross.   Psalm 109:24
10. His hands and feet would be pierced.   Psalm 22:16
11. He would die between two thieves.   Isaiah 53:12
12. He would bear shame, reproach and dishonor.   Psalm 69:19
13. He would pray for His executioners. Isaiah 53:12; Psalm 109:4
14. People would shake their heads at Him.   Psalms 109:25; 22:7
15. He would be ridiculed.   Psalm 22:8
16. People would be astonished.   Psalm 22:17; Isaiah 52:14
17. His garments would be parted
    and lots would be cast for them.   Psalm 22:18
18. He would thirst.   Psalm 69:3
19. He would be given gall and vinegar to drink.   Psalm 69:21
20. He would cry out, "My God,
    my God, why hast thou forsaken me?"   Psalm 22:1

21. He would commit his soul to God.   Psalm 31:5
22. He would give a cry of victory and triumph.   Psalm 22:31
23. His friends would stand far off.   Psalm 38:11
24. His bones would not be broken.   Psalm 34:20; Exodus 12:46
25. His side would be pierced.   Zechariah 12:10
26. His visage would be marred.   Isaiah 52:14
27. His heart would be broken.   Psalm 22:14
28. Darkness would cover the land.   Amos 8:9
29. He would be buried in a rich man's tomb.   Isaiah 53:9
30. He would be cut off, but not for himself.   Daniel 9:26
31. He would be the Lamb of God.   Isaiah 53:7

The odds against any one man fulfilling all thirty-one of these prophecies is staggering:

1 chance in 431,696,000

But Jesus did. We can read in the New Testament the accounts of Jesus' last day and see that He did. But He also fulfilled another prophecy, the most important one of all: God was to raise him from the dead (Ps. 16:10).

Jesus not only fulfilled all of these thirty-two prophecies, but during His lifetime on earth He fulfilled all of the Old Testament prophecies, over 300 of them. [1]

The odds against one man doing this in one lifetime is:

1 chance in 8×10^{132}

To illustrate just how large this number is, let's put in the zeros.

1 chance in 8x1,000,000,000,000,000,000,000,000,000,000
000,000,000,000,000,000,000,000,000,000
000,000,000,000,000,000,000,000,000,000
000,000,000,000,000,000,000,000,000,000

Astonishing odds, but Jesus did it. He did it because the prophecies were made by men who were God's prophets speaking for God, and He was truly the one being prophesied about — the Son of God.

The prophecy made in John's book of Revelation will also come about because John was also God's prophet and the revelation was made directly to John by Jesus Christ, and this confirms prophecy made in the Old Testament by other prophets of God.

The antichrist will fulfill all of the prophecy made about him. He has no choice in the matter, for God is in control of all events in this world and He has ordained that this prophecy come to pass. It is necessary for all this to be accomplished in order that Jesus Christ may return to earth and reclaim the prize He won by defeating Satan on the cross.

What we in the world will see in the end times is a physical manifestation of a spiritual war fought between the forces of good and the forces of evil. It is a war between God and Satan.

Paul wrote "For we wrestle not against flesh and blood, but against principalities, against powers, against the rulers of the darkness of this world, against spiritual wickedness in high places" (Eph. 6:12).

This is exactly what is taking shape in the world today. The final battle is about to take place, and we are not just spectators but participants in it.

How accurate has biblical prophecy been? How seriously are we to take the Revelation prophecy concerning the antichrist and the end times of this world?

Everything predicted in the Bible has actually happened — except the events of the end times. We should take them very seriously — for they are serious matters.

Deadly serious!

9

What Will He Do?

We have grasped the mystery of the atom and rejected the Sermon on the Mount. (Omar Bradley)

He that strives to touch the stars oft stumbles at a straw. (Edmund Spenser)

If Mikhail S. Gorbachev is truly the antichrist John wrote about, it should be possible to predict with a relatively high degree of accuracy from biblical prophecy and from the current shape of world conditions what he will do to fulfill the Revelation prophecy.

One point strikes home with terrible reality: what the prophecy states that the antichrist will accomplish in the end times is *exactly* the expressed goals and objectives of international communism. This is *complete world domination.*

This is by no means a coincidence. Satan has been in control of the Soviet Union ever since the country was established in 1917 by the communist takeover. The world bears sad witness to the militant expansion of Soviet power after World War II and the exporting of the communist revolution to all parts of the globe.

Let us examine what the Revelation prophecy tells us about what the antichrist will do to achieve world conquest and determine the sequence of events which are likely to occur in order to fulfill this prophecy.

"And I saw, and behold a white horse: and he that sat on him had a bow; and a crown was given unto him: and he went forth conquering and to conquer" (Rev. 6:2).

Throughout history, conquerors have almost always been pictured astride a white stallion. This has been the historical image of a great conqueror, and this is exactly how John sees the antichrist.

The man John sees sitting on the white horse has a bow, the symbol of military power. Gorbachev certainly has a bow — the most powerful bow in all of history is the Soviet and Communist bloc military machine. This military power is completely under his control and command.

A crown was given to the man on the white horse. Gorbachev was given his crown on March 11, 1985. He wears the crown of the Soviet Union.

The Extent of His Conquest

Revelation 13:7 tells us what this conqueror will accomplish, "And it was given unto him to make war with the saints, and to overcome them: and power was given him over all kindreds, and tongues, and nations."

He will make war with the 'saints' and will defeat them. He will conquer and rule the entire world. If Gorbachev is truly the antichrist, he will accomplish something no man in history before him has been able to do — he will conquer the whole world.

This is in evidence by what the prophecy says; he will have power over *all* kindreds and tongues and nations. He will rule the entire world.

Nebuchadnezzar's empire was vast and Babylon controlled most of the civilized world. The Persians extended this, but they ruled only from the boundary of Europe to that of India. Alexander greatly enlarged this, but certainly did not control the entire earth. Caesar extended Rome's empire to include parts of mainland Europe and the British Isles, but in no way did the Roman Empire cover the globe. But *the antichrist's rule will encompass the entire earth!*

All nations will be at his feet. All people in the world will be subject to him. At last Satan, through the antichrist, will actually be in complete control of the population of the earth.

War With the Saints

We are told in this part of the Revelation prophecy that he will make war with the saints and overcome them. Who are these 'saints' against whom he will make war?

To answer this we have only to look at the nations which oppose the Soviet Union. These are, by and large, the Christian nations of the world and most of them are members of NATO. I believe the 'saints' in this prophecy are the citizens of the United States, Canada, England and the mainland nations of Western Europe.

There are other Christian countries in the world, such as Australia, New Zealand, South Africa and the nations of South and Central America, but these countries do not have sufficient military strength to pose any serious threat to the antichrist's conquest of the world. In fact, there is *only one thing* standing in the way of the Soviet world domination — the American nuclear deterrent. In the analysis of what the antichrist will do to achieve world domination, everything else must be secondary to the elimination of the American nuclear deterrent from the path of the Soviet Union's quest to control the world.

This is, today, the single most important factor preventing the red flag of communism from flying over all the capitals of the nations of the earth. The elimination of this will dictate the strategy of the antichrist and the Soviet Union and all that they do will have a direct bearing upon achieving this. But they will achieve it, and I believe there will be help coming from several other sources which will take the power and military might of the United States completely out of the picture in the last days of this earth.

But What About Red China?

Any discussion concerning the Soviet Union's domination of the world has to take into account the People's Republic of China, the most populous nation on earth. With one billion people, China is home for 20 percent of the world's population.

In spite of the relaxed atmosphere between the United States and Red China, we must always bear in mind that world domination by communism remains the ultimate goal of all communists, who use peace only as long as it serves their ultimate goals. Trade and friendly relations with the West happen to be in the best interests of the

Chinese communists today. Tomorrow may well be another story, especially when the American nuclear deterrent is no longer in existence and there is nothing to prevent Soviet worldwide expansion and domination. China remains under Marxist doctrine, despite its seemingly relaxed state. The aims of communism have not changed one iota for all of the trade and cultural exchange with the West.

Red China will play an important role in end-times events and this is prophesied in this book of Revelation. The Red Chinese Army will take part in the Battle of Armageddon, as we shall see when we get to that chapter later in this book.

Since Red China also possesses nuclear weapons, the antichrist cannot control the entire earth if these weapons pose a threat to his supremacy. There will be two courses of action possible for Gorbachev, if he is truly the antichrist: to heal the ideological rift with Red China and have them as partners in world conquest, or to eliminate the Chinese nuclear arsenal by a preemptive first strike.

China is one country in the world with an excellent chance to survive a nuclear war. If all the major Chinese cities were completely destroyed by nuclear annihilation, only 10 percent of the Chinese population would be killed. This would still leave over 900 million Chinese alive, more than enough to mobilize the largest army the world has ever seen with which to participate in the Battle of Armageddon.

The Revelation prophecy tells us in no uncertain terms that the antichrist will have power over *all* kindreds, tongues and nations. This must include China, whose population totals 20 percent of the earth's people.

The Worship of the Whole World

Another prophecy which tells us that the antichrist will control the entire earth is found in Revelation 13:8: "And all that dwell upon the earth shall worship him, whose names are not written in the book of life of the lamb slain from the foundation of the world."

Here is that word *'all'* again. All, except the dedicated Christians whose names are written in the Book of Life. He will be the god of all people in the world. For a short time Satan will have achieved his master plan, and those who worship the antichrist will actually be worshiping Satan, his master.

The War of Peace

We must remember that the primary obstacle in the path of Soviet world domination is the American nuclear deterrent. Not only must the American-based ICBM's be taken out of the way, but the nuclear weapons the U.S.-NATO forces have in Europe must be eliminated. This will be the first step in the War of Peace, getting the American Pershing II, Cruise, and tactical nuclear weapons off European soil.

The Western World, and especially the European nations, are anxious for the United States and the Soviet Union to agree on nuclear disarmament. Gorbachev has already offered to remove his SS-20 missiles from Europe in exchange for the removal of American missiles. As the SS-20's are targeted on cities of our NATO allies, they will encourage such an agreement. This has already been hailed as a possible first step in nuclear disarmament between the two superpowers.

The Reagan presidency has been seriously damaged by the Iran-Contra affair. This situation adds impetus to the administration's desire to conclude a nuclear arms reduction treaty with the Soviet Union in order to create an event which will overshadow the disturbing affairs which have highlighted the last years of Ronald Reagan's second term. Naturally enough, any president desires to be remembered in history for positive contributions to his country. The elimination of short-range and medium-range nuclear weapons would certainly be an accomplishment to be remembered by the American people, whether it actually increases the stability of peace in the world or has just the opposite effect.

Gorbachev is anxious to present himself to the world as a man of peace, to be trusted and accepted by the Western World. Such a treaty would establish him as the leading global statesman of the age. He would be hailed by the entire world community as 'a man of peace.' I expect such treaties to be signed before the end of the current administration and to result in what will be a monumental victory for Gorbachev and the Soviet Union.

(Editor's note: Before this book went to press, a treaty to eliminate all intermediate range missiles was signed by Secretary Gorbachev and President Reagan. Plans have also been made for another summit in Moscow with the objective of reducing strategic missiles by 50 percent.)

The irony of all this is that Gorbachev, the man who is very probably the antichrist, could conceivably be awarded the Nobel Peace Prize, along with Ronald Reagan who will retire from office with dignity and respect for it.

What irony this will be, for if Gorbachev is truly the man John saw astride a white horse with a bow and a crown, he will, as told to us in Revelation 6:3, "go forth conquering and to conquer."

And in Revelation 6:4, "...and power was given to him that sat thereon to take peace from the earth, and that they should kill one another: and there was given unto him a great sword."

Gorbachev has already proposed a plan to eliminate all nuclear weapons in the world by the year 2000. He is a master at worldwide public relations, and the Soviet Union is using Western-style tactics of publicity to build his image as a seeker of world peace. At future summit meetings, the United States, and its president, will be under considerable pressure to conclude such a treaty, with some type of limited nuclear reduction immediately — possibly the reduction or withdrawal of U.S. weapons from Europe in exchange for something similar by the Soviets.

(Editor's note: The Washington summit meeting in December, 1987, between Gorbachev and Reagan proved to be a public relations victory for Gorbachev. The worldwide media coverage of this event elevated Gorbachev's status of a respected world leader to the point that in Europe the polls show that he is considered to be more trustworthy than President Reagan by a wide majority. His status at home was also greatly improved, consolidating his power base with the Soviet people and Kremlin leaders.)

The removal of U.S. nuclear weapons from Europe is essential to the Soviet overall game plan. The Soviet Union cannot allow a nuclear war to be fought in Europe. The Chernobyl nuclear accident released only a miniscule amount of radiation into the atmosphere compared to that caused by a nuclear weapon's detonation. But even this small amount contaminated a section of Soviet farmland which was the richest in the nation. The Soviets cannot feed the Russian population now and the contamination of vast amounts of farmland would result in a national catastrophe of unprecedented magnitude.

Soviet industry is unable to supply the basic needs of the Soviet people in relation to what they see in the West. Only the addition of the industrial complexes of Western Europe would raise the standard of living of the Russian people to what they would be satisfied with in the future. The complaints of those behind the Iron Curtain have increased dramatically of late as they have seen the great disparity between the communist standard of living and that of the Free World. Gorbachev can not risk the destruction of either Soviet agricultural land nor the industry of the West by a nuclear war in Europe.

As much as the Soviet government has tried to prevent it, their young people are listening to Western-style music, buying designer jeans in the black market, and wearing T-shirts bearing Western slogans. Gorbachev has promised to raise the standard of Soviet living and increase the quantity of consumer goods. He will have to make good on these promises before the complaints grow into something more serious.

Other Prophecy He Will Fulfill

In his War of Peace with the West, Gorbachev will be used by God to fulfill another end-times prophecy. Ezekiel foretold of Jews being scattered into all the Gentile nations, but he also prophesied that in the last days they would be brought back to Israel from the far corners of the earth. In Ezekiel 36:24, we read, "For I will take you from among the heathen, and gather you out of all countries, and will bring you into your own land."

Notice that God has promised to bring them back from *all* countries. As of now, Jews from every nation in the world — but one — who desired to go to Israel have been allowed to return. That exception is the Soviet Union. There are hundreds of thousands of Jews there who would go to Israel if they were allowed to leave. Many have applied for exit visas and have been refused. More would apply but when a Jew has filed for this visa and has been refused, he risks suffering horrible consequences that include the loss of his job and living quarters. Not many today will risk that in the face of almost certain refusal.

But God has promised they would come back from *all* countries. I expect to see the reestablishment of diplomatic relations between Israel and the Soviet Union — and, as a result, all Jews desiring to emigrate to Israel will be allowed to leave.

This is not the first time God will have used the atheistic Soviet Union to fulfill biblical prophecy.

The Soviet Union Helped Establish Israel

God used the Soviet Union to help in the establishment of the State of Israel in fulfillment of biblical prophecy concerning the end times.

The Russians have long been aware of the strategic value of the oil-rich Middle East. At the end of World War II, British influence was very strong there. Great Britain had governed Palestine under the mandate given after the termination of the First World War and had trained and equipped the Arab armies which would be the military power after the British left. The Arab Legions of Jordan were considered to be the best-trained and most-formidable military force in the area.

The Soviets had tried to get a foot in the door of the Middle East in 1946 when they invaded the Azerbaijan region of Iran. But under British and American threats, they had been forced to withdraw. As a result, the Shah of Iran became a staunch American ally and any hopes of Soviet influence in Iran faded. But the United Nations gave them another opportunity, and they sought to remedy the situation in another place.

The Soviet role in the establishment of the State of Israel is not well-known and little mention is made of it, but it was Soviet pressure in the United Nations which resulted in the resolution leading to the founding of Israel as an independent nation in 1948. The Russians fully expected that this new and weak nation would welcome Soviet aid and would become an ally in the Middle East, offsetting the West's position with Iran and other Arab countries, thus establishing a firm Soviet foothold among the oil-producing Third World countries.

No sooner had the proclamation of Israeli independence been read than the Arab armies attacked. The British had managed to turn over their arms and ammunition to the Arabs, leaving Israel virtually defenseless. The Soviet Union quickly stepped in, arranging the sale and delivery of badly needed arms through Czechoslovakia just in time to prevent Israel from being overwhelmed by the well-equipped Arab forces.

But the Israelis were no fools. They could see the motives behind the aid and turned to the United States and its large and affluent Jewish population for assistance. Israel has since become one of the staunchest allies of this country.

The fact remains that God used the Soviet Union to fulfill this prophecy of the reestablishment of the Jewish homeland in the end times. He will also use them to fulfill the prophecy concerning the return of *all* Jews (from *all* nations) who desire to return to their ancient home. The antichrist will allow them to return for a different motive, but the prophecy will indeed be fulfilled.

Middle East Oil and the Antichrist's Plans

The modern technological world runs on oil. Even an agricultural nation cannot survive without it, for most of the modern pesticides and fertilizers utilize it as a raw material. Transportation on land, sea and in the air fully depend on oil. Without it, no nation can long survive.

The Soviet Union is, at present, an oil-exporting country, but it has been forecast that within ten years the Soviets will be forced to import oil to keep Russian industry moving. Oil is a vital ingredient in the plans of the Soviet Union and the antichrist.

The Soviet Union has found its plans to be totally unsuccessful in the Middle East by using client nations. Rebuffed by Israel, Iran and Egypt, the Soviet Union will not rely on surrogates in the future. The next move of the Soviet Union will be by the Red Army itself, and the new bases in southern Afghanistan will provide the jumping-off points.

Middle East oil must pass through two 'choke points' in the tankers which carry this oil to both Asia and the Western world. One of these narrow straits is located between the Persian Gulf and the Arabian Sea. This is the very strategic Strait of Hormuz. On a straight line from new Soviet bases in Afghanistan, Russian tanks are only 350 miles from this important narrows, through which much of the free world's oil must pass. This will mean a Soviet invasion of Iran, but there will be no way Iranian forces can stop this thrust by Soviet armor.

The other 'choke point' is through the narrow opening between the Red Sea and the Gulf of Aden. The Soviets have this narrows outflanked on both sides; by bases in Ethiopia on the African side and by bases in the communist-controlled People's Democratic Republic of Yemen across the strait in Asia. Soviet planes and ships could easily cut this lifeline of oil from flowing to the West.

When the time comes in the plans of the antichrist, both of these oil routes will be cut off, while the oil-producing nations of the Middle East will supply the Soviet Union with all the oil necessary to maintain Soviet industry and military needs.

The United States has tried to counter these Soviet moves by establishing a military base in Oman, but at the present time this is only a standby operation, with no American fighting forces stationed there. In the event of war, the U.S. has stockpiled ammunition and weapons and has built a large airfield, but Oman has been reluctant to allow an actual American military presence here for fear of retaliation. With no means of defending this base actually there, the Soviets could easily neutralize or even capture this important base by use of an airborne strike with one of the many Soviet airborne divisions.

The Soviet Union has increased its navy substantially in the past years. With the withdrawal of American forces from South Vietnam, the Russians moved portions of their Pacific fleet into the U.S.-built naval base at Camrahn Bay. The Soviet fleet is ready to challenge the U.S. Navy in the Pacific and is within striking distance of the American base at Subic Bay in the Philippines. The Pacific is no longer an 'American lake.'

The Plan for Africa

The Soviet Union has made great strides in subverting new and emerging African countries. The worldwide communist fight against 'imperialists' has forced the independence of many new African nations who were totally unprepared to take over self-government and deal with communist infiltration and subversion at the same time.

As much as one abhors racism and the racially restrictive policies in South Africa, the fact remains that the white South African government and military force is the lone deterrent against a complete African takeover by the Soviet Union, and the deterrent is very much in jeopardy at the present time.

There is no doubt regarding who is funding the terrorist and 'liberation' forces at work in South Africa. It is no secret that the communist influence in the ANC and other organizations is substantial. Now, with world opinion very much against the South African government, attempting to force changes in that country for black participation in government, the question is not if, but when the bloodbath will take place.

When the communist led, backed and armed revolt takes place in South Africa, the entire continent will fall into Soviet-controlled hands. I can see nothing that will be able to stop this eventuality from occurring.

South America — Potential Powder Keg

The Soviet Union got its first foothold in the Western Hemisphere in 1959 when the Batista regime was overthrown by rebels under Fidel Castro and the left-wingers in the movement assumed control of the country. Krushchev attempted to install nuclear missiles in Cuba in 1962, but was forced to withdraw them when President Kennedy stood firm, threatening war if they remained. This was one of the points which led to Krushchev's downfall.

But in later years, the Soviet buildup has been largely ignored and it is known that there are Soviet combat troops in Cuba at the present time, as well as Soviet bombers and fighters. The United States has not challenged this Soviet presence in Cuba, only ninety miles from American shores.

The greatest service Cuba has provided for the Soviet Union has been as the base for the export of communist revolution into Central and South America, as well as the use of surrogate Cuban combat troops in Soviet takeovers in Africa. Nicaragua has been their greatest success to date, but communist rebels are active in El Salvador and other Central American countries.

The Soviet Union, through its client, Cuba, has made great inroads into Mexico, which has been openly critical of American policy and totally uncooperative in many important matters. Relations between the United States and Mexico will further deteriorate as the economy of Mexico, which has been teetering on the verge of collapse, finally comes crashing down. We will discuss the effects of this later when we deal with the coming world financial disasters that loom on the horizon.

Gorbachev will attempt to draw American troops into the fighting in Central America — to create another situation similar to our involvement in Vietnam.

Gorbachev's Consolidation of Power

Since assuming power in March of 1985, Mikhail S. Gorbachev has moved very quickly to consolidate that power and strengthen his hand. He has revised the Politburo, getting rid of those members who opposed his views and replacing them with his own people — those who would be completely loyal to the General Secretary and his policies.

One of the first to go was Andrei Gromyko, Foreign Minister, who was replaced by Eduard Shevardnadze — a man who had absolutely no experience or training in foreign affairs but was totally Gorbachev's man. Gromyko was made President of the Soviet Union, a post which is ceremonial only, with no political power whatsoever.

Shevardnadze is an organization man who will reflect Gorbachev's own position at all times without question. But Gorbachev needed a man who knew the United States intimately. He recalled Anatoly Dobrynin from his post as ambassador to the United States and made him a personal advisor, installing Dobrynin in the prestigious Communist Party Central Committee.

Gorbachev has shaken up the military as well as the political structure of the Soviet Union. Chernenko had fired Marshal Nickolai Ogarkov during his brief tenure as head of the Soviet Union. Gorbachev brought him back as commander of the Warsaw Pact Forces and also made him Deputy Defense Minister. Ogarkov is known as a 'hard liner' and is just the type of man Gorbachev will need when he must call on the Warsaw Pact Forces to carry out his plans in Europe.

When the 27th Communist Party Congress met in March of 1986, Gorbachev continued to purge the dead wood and those who opposed his plans. At least half of the delegates to the 27th Congress were relieved of their jobs and will no longer represent their home districts. He replaced these with people who will unquestionably carry out his orders, no matter what they might be.

Gorbachev also fired other senior military men. The branch of the Soviet military machine which controls Soviet nuclear missiles is the Strategic Rocket Forces. He fired Marshal Vladimir Tolubko as head of that most important force and replaced him with a man who will obey his orders without question. Also fired was General Alexei Yepichev, political chief of the Soviet Armed Forces.

Make no mistake about it, Mikhail S. Gorbachev is now firmly in control of the political, military and ideological aspects of the Soviet Union.

Star Wars — A Bogus Bargaining Chip

In 1972 the United States and the Soviet Union signed the Strategic Arms Limitations Talks agreement, known as SALT I. This agreement was to assure that both nations were vulnerable to destruction by nuclear armed ICBMs so that neither nation would dare use them first. This treaty limited antiballistic missile sites to one in each country and to 100 antiballistic missiles. It also expressly prohibited deployment of radar or other warning systems which could be used to direct antiballistic missiles. Other provisions of this treaty froze the numbers of both land-based and submarine-based ICBMs at: U.S. — 1,054 ICBMs and 656 SLBMs and the USSR at 1,400 ICBMs and 950 SLBMs.

In September of 1977 the U.S. and the Soviet Union agreed to continue to abide by this treaty even though it had expired after five years.

But the Russians had *never* lived up to this agreement. No sooner had the ink dried on this treaty back in 1972 than the Soviet Union had begun construction of the huge Krasnoyarsk radar installation. This type of 'horizontal' radar is explicitly banned by SALT I because it can detect missiles as soon as they are fired from the U.S. and can be used to direct antiballistic missiles to intercept them. The purpose of SALT I was to keep each side vulnerable to assure the concept of Mutually Assured Destruction, known as MAD.

The reason the Soviets wasted no time in beginning construction of the Krasnoyarsk radar was that it was the item with the longest lead time in their plans to have a Strategic Defense Initiative in place and fully operational without the United States becoming aware of its existence. The Russians, who call President Reagan's Star Wars plan 'immoral,' have been constructing their own for many years.

The huge radar complex at Krasnoyarsk went undetected for years by American spy satellites. It was only when a Soviet defector informed the CIA that such an installation was being built there that we reexamined photographs taken by satellite and confirmed his story. This reveals the unreliability of our space-based detection of what the Soviets are doing. To compound our problems, the shuttle disaster in January of 1986 and the subsequent failure of the Delta and other rockets to launch additional spy satellites has just about made us totally blind, with only one of the latest state-of-the-art satellites now in orbit.

Sixty-four legal ABMs ring Moscow. We do not know how many others are hidden, for the Soviet Union has never honored any treaty it has signed. In addition, there are at least 11,000 Soviet ground-to-air missiles deployed in 1,650 sites within the Soviet Union, and many more in the Warsaw Pact countries. These missiles are effective against aircraft operating at between 2,000 and 80,000 feet. There are also batteries of SA-3 missiles which are effective against lower-flying aircraft. In addition, the Soviets have an estimated 2,600 jet interceptor aircraft, many with all-weather capabilities.

The Russians have screamed loud and long against the proposed Star Wars system of the Untied States. But they have themselves been carrying out the very research and development they are calling immoral and are possibly very close to having some of it in place. Research on laser and particle beams for this purpose began years ago in the Soviet Union and they are far in advance of us in the development and deployment of these antiballistic, space-oriented systems.

Gorbachev's Bait-and-Switch Plan

Gorbachev has made much to do over the American Star Wars system. At first, he had even stated that additional summit meetings would depend on the American willingness to negotiate on this item and delay deployment far into the future. But I do not believe that Gorbachev is one bit worried about the American Star Wars system. He is using this as a gambit in the old bait-and-switch con game.

What Gorbachev wants is the removal of U.S. nuclear weapons from Europe. When the summit talks get down to the nitty-gritty, he will switch off on his demands concerning Star Wars — in exchange for removal of American nuclear weapons from Europe. His whole game plan depends on achieving this.

Gorbachev's Game Plan for the War of Peace

In the years just ahead we will see Gorbachev's strategy unfold while he and the Soviet Union wage their War of Peace against the

United States and the Free World. We have touched on some of these points in this chapter. Now let's organize them into what might be called his game plan for conducting this war of diplomacy — and subversion.

Gorbachev's number-one priority is the removal of American nuclear weapons from Europe. Everything else he does is secondary to this, for we shall see in a later chapter that his subsequent moves —after the War against the Saints begins — will depend on there being no American nuclear weapons on European soil.

In order to accomplish this, Gorbachev will come to the bargaining table protesting the U.S. Strategic Defense Initiative, but very willing to trade this off to get U.S. nuclear weapons out of Europe. He may well tie this in with overall reduction in long-range weapons, ICBMs, but without a means of verifying Soviet compliance, this will amount to nothing. But the United States will be under great pressure to accomplish *something* in terms of nuclear disarmament, and we will likely end up with the very short end of the stick.

The Soviets will increase their subversion, direct and indirect, in South America, Africa and Asia. William J. Casey, former director of the CIA, now deceased, stated in a rare public speech that Mikhail S. Gorbachev and the Soviet Union have intensified their efforts to secure "bridgeheads for spreading subversion and extending Soviet influence in the Middle East, Central America and Africa."

Casey said, "The Sandanista government of Nicaragua started an all-out campaign to destroy the U.S.-backed Contras, including driving thousands of Miskito Indians across the border. Cuban troops and Soviet advisors in Angola are feverishly preparing a campaign, likely to be launched very soon, designed to wipe out the forces resisting the Marxist government of Angola."

Casey blasted the Soviet General Secretary, "We have a new Soviet leader, Mr. Gorbachev, and already a hallmark of his regime is an intensified effort to nail down and cement these bridgeheads, make them permanent. Today we are witnessing particularly intensive efforts to tilt the overall strategic balance against the West." (Speech before the Annual Conference of the American Israel Public Affairs Committee.)

The Soviet Union will reestablish diplomatic relations with Israel. As a conciliatory gesture, Soviet Jews will be allowed to leave and emigrate to Israel. The reason behind this is that Gorbachev wants a part in any peace talks and subsequent settlement between Israel and the Palestinians with regard to a Palestinian homeland. This would become immediately a Soviet-client state and give Gorbachev a solid footing and position in the heart of the Middle East.

Soviet espionage will greatly increase in the United States. This has already occurred, and the arrest of a few Americans who sold secret information to the KGB is but the tip of the iceberg as far as Soviet spying is concerned.

On top of the Soviet shopping list is information about the newest electronic methods of detecting and locating nuclear submarines. This may have already been seriously compromised and they may already have this information.

Although our nuclear submarines are capable of remaining submerged for long periods of time, they can theoretically be located by very sophisticated detection systems carried by orbiting satellites. A diesel-electric submarine can lie on the bottom of the sea silently, all engines completely turned off. But a nuclear-powered submarine cannot easily shut down its nuclear reactor, and as long as the reactor is critical it requires large amounts of cooling water. This is pumped into the reactor from the sea and is discharged at a slightly higher temperature. It is technically possible to design a highly sensitive satellite system which can detect the very slight warming of the water around a nuclear submarine due to the discharge of the cooling water from its reactor. Soviet spies may well have obtained our research in this field and be constructing such a satellite system right now.

Another priority of Gorbachev is to project his personal image to the world as a 'man of peace.' He will do everything possible to accomplish this, while the United States will be portrayed as the war monger, the nation most likely to start the nuclear holocaust which could incinerate the entire world. At the time of talks between the Soviet leader and the American president, 'spontaneous' peace demonstrations will occur in various parts of the world, demanding that the United States give in to the Soviet proposals for reduction and eventual elimination of nuclear arms.

The War against the Saints and the subsequent conquest of the world by Gorbachev, if he is truly the antichrist, cannot happen until several other events take place. One is the removal of American nuclear weapons from Europe. Another is the release of Soviet Jews who desire to return to their homeland in Israel.

The big event — and the one from which we will begin counting the antichrist's remaining time in power — will be the appearance and healing of "the deadly wound." This will mark the end of the War of Peace and the beginning of a period of hell on earth.

10

The Coming World Crisis

For my thoughts are not your thoughts, neither are your ways my ways. (Isaiah 55:8)

It isn't the experience of today that drives men mad. It is the remorse for something that happened yesterday and the dread of what tomorrow may bring. (Robert Jones Burdette)

In the immediate future, in the last stages of the period which Christ called "the time of sorrows" and the beginning of the antichrist's War with the Saints, the world will steadily plummet into a crisis never before experienced.

World Economic Collapse

The state of the world's economy is teetering on the verge of a catastrophic financial collapse. The developed nations of the Western World have loaned enormous amounts of money they cannot afford to lose to the underdeveloped Third World who cannot afford to pay it back.

If the bulk of this money had been spent wisely, there would be a lesser problem, but the governments of these Third World nations have squandered these loans on worthless projects or in military buildups which contribute absolutely nothing to the nation's ability to repay these loans.

The International Monetary Fund and the World Bank are the two international lenders to whom the Third World nations owe substantial amounts of money. But private banks have heavily invested in the developing countries as well, and it is these private banks that will be hit hardest when the house of cards comes tumbling down.

American banks in particular rushed to the capitals of these Third World countries, eager to lend them all the money they wanted — at interest rates considerably higher than they would be able to get from any other borrowers. As most of these countries were newly rich in oil, the investments seemed safe. After all, oil was selling at over thirty dollars per barrel and the revenues were pouring into these once-impoverished countries and promising to soon make them the wealthiest nations on the earth.

The debts of these fifty-six African, Latin American and Caribbean countries is now a monumental $415 billion, $370 billion of which is owed by South American nations and Mexico. But the bubble burst when the glut of oil dropped the price by two-thirds, and the payments on these loans came due.

Mexico alone has a foreign debt of about $100 billion, and cannot make even the interest payments. This fact, and related economic conditions, have caused panic in the world financial community.

The creditors had but one choice, and see for yourself just what.a hole they have dug for themselves. They loaned Mexico the money with which to pay the interest, further adding to the total on which that country would have to pay even more interest, postponing the ultimate and inevitable day of reckoning when the Mexican government will have to declare bankruptcy and disavow all debts.

The Mexican government is now pressing for a stretched-out repayment schedule and a reduction of the interest rates. With the threat of bankruptcy and the prospect of losing their entire investment, the banks will probably give in to this. But if they reduce the rates for Mexico, they will have to do the same with the other debtors. What looked initially like wonderfully profitable loans have suddenly turned into an assorted collection of cans of worms.

When these loans are defaulted, not *if* but *when*, the effect on American banks will be catastrophic. Some of these American banks are already much overextended, loaning out as much as seventeen times their capitalization. When Mexico goes under, she will take some of the largest American banking institutions with her.

Mexico is not the only Latin American nation in severe trouble. Brazil, the largest debtor with over $104 billion is in similar trouble. Argentina's debt is $49 billion; Venezuela's debt $32 billion; Peru has a $14 billion indebtedness, and these nations have recently met together to call for more lenient terms from western banks.

Lenders are trying to hold off this collapse until the debtor nations who are also oil producers again reap the profits from expensive crude oil on the world market. No one expects the price of oil to remain at its current depressed price. This would probably work out, except for one factor which is beyond their control — the Saudis won't let that happen.

The Saudi Plan for World Oil Control

The largest reserves of oil in the world remain undisturbed beneath the torrid sands of the Arabian desert. When the proven reserves of most of the world are exhausted, the Saudis will still be pumping oil.

With a glut of oil on the world market that has reduced the price of crude to as low as nine dollars a barrel, one would certainly expect Saudi Arabia to cut production in order to again balance the supply and demand, thereby increasing the price of oil to what it was a few years ago. Americans, and the world's oil consumers, have not questioned the motive behind the refusal of the Saudis to do this. After all, cheap gasoline has been welcomed by American motorists and homeowners who heat with oil have breathed a sigh of relief over heating bills. Why, then, has Saudi Arabia taken this course? It seems to make no sense!

But it does make sense to the Saudis. Saudi Arabian oil can be extracted for about two dollars a barrel. Mexican oil costs four dollars; U.S. domestic oil costs eight dollars and North Sea oil costs a walloping sixteen dollars a barrel to produce. The longer the oil glut continues, with the price greatly depressed, the harder these countries will be strapped. Many of the smaller oil-producing nations will go bankrupt — the once-lucrative oil revenues no longer capable of sustaining the country's heavy foreign indebtedness. By about 1990, these small and economically stressed countries will no longer be in competition with Saudi Arabia and several other major OPEC oil producers.

When that happens, former oil prices of thirty dollars to thirty-five dollars a barrel will be reinstated and the price will go up drastically from there — perhaps reaching fifty dollars a barrel or more. Saudi Arabia will become the richest nation in the world.

But it won't be for long. With the combination of defaulting Third World nations and the astronomical price of oil, the world will be quickly thrown into the deepest depression in history. No nation in the world will be unaffected by it.

A Bankrupt America

For over a decade the United States has maintained its standard of living by deficit spending. The reason why we have gotten away with this so far is that foreign money has been invested in this country because of two things: high interest rates here, and the relative safety of investing in the United States. But this will not last long once the Third World begins defaulting on loans made by American banks, forcing many of the largest financial institutions into bankruptcy.

American interest rates have already declined, and could decrease even further, making investments here less attractive to foreign money. Petrodollars have principally kept the American economy afloat even with huge deficit spending, but the time of reckoning is coming fast and the results will be disastrous.

The world economy is very much like a house of cards, with the United States as the keystone card. A recession in the United States is felt worldwide. A depression here will certainly have a cataclysmic effect on the economy of the entire world. When America's economy suffers a twinge of pain, many small countries of the world double over in agony. But when this depression strikes America, economic and political chaos will result in many of the nations of the earth.

The Mexican economy is hanging by a thread. Within the next few years, when that thread breaks, a new and horrendous problem will confront America. Conditions will get so bad in Mexico that millions of Mexicans will flee and they will run to the only country which can feed them — the United States. This vast horde of illegal immigrants will flood across the border and we will be powerless to stop them. We will also be powerless to send them back. States such as Texas, California, Arizona, New Mexico and nearby ones will be flooded with homeless, hungry, impoverished people. The American moral sense will make it impossible to ignore the needs of these people. The government, along with private groups, will have to feed, house, clothe, and take care of these refugees which could very well number over ten million. How much will this cost in an economy already staggering with debt? At a very conservative estimate of $3,000 per person per year, the cost would be at least thirty billion dollars.

Political Chaos

Many nations, especially in Central and South America, are experiencing political difficulties now, with communist rebels active in remote provinces, waging guerilla warfare against government troops. The deep economic problems felt in these countries will attract many young people to their cause and will certainly result in political chaos, with some of these governments falling to communist-controlled insurrectionists.

It is highly possible that even our close neighbor to the south, Mexico, could fall under leftist control — with help from both Cuba and Nicaragua and funded by the Soviet Union.

World Famine — Is It Possible?

There is no shortage of food in the world today. In fact, there is a surplus of food in the world. The nations experiencing famine, such as Ethiopia, are starving because of poverty, not because of a shortage of food. Climatic conditions have certainly affected the ability of these people to grow crops locally, but they suffer because they cannot afford food, not because of a lack of it in the world.

The Western plains of the United States contain the world's largest bread-basket. The usual bumper crops grown there produce the surplus of food in the world. Canada, Australia and Argentina also grow more grain than can be used domestically and these nations also contribute greatly to the abundance of food. But in the very near future this may not be so, and the world may well suffer because of it.

The past 6,000 years have coincided with the warmest period the earth has experienced in 100,000 years. There have been ups and downs within that time, but none has been so severe as to threaten the earth's population. The last century was a cold one. But since the early 1900's, the earth's climate has been extraordinarily benign and balmy. This continued until about 1940 when the trend turned downward. It has accelerated since then.

One of the most interesting theories concerning this change in the weather pattern concerns the increased amount of dust — both man-made and from volcanic activity. Volcanoes, unusually dormant since the turn of the century, have been acting up again significantly since 1955. The eruption of Mount St. Helens is but one example of long-dormant volcanoes suddenly coming to life.

Most climatologists agree that a decrease of only 1 percent in sunlight would be sufficient to cause radical changes in the earth's climate. The larger temperature differential between the equator and the poles is causing a shifting of the vital, monsoon-bearing winds and the change in turbulence of the atmosphere has already brought climate changes to some parts of the world.

Monitoring stations around the world have reported measurable increases in the amount of dust in the atmosphere with a corresponding decrease in its transparency which has reduced the amount of direct sunlight reaching the earth. In a belt stretching from Africa through Pakistan and India, and into some parts of China, there have been widespread changes in rainfall, resulting in drought in some areas and increased flooding and damaging tropical storms in others. Scientists agree that the earth's climate is changing — and it is apt to get much worse.

In the United States this change in the weather is already noticeable. Winters are getting colder much farther south than in any time in this century. Many fear a return to the climate of the 1800s when heavy snows and bitter cold were common as far south as the Gulf Coast. Except for the West Coast, the entire United States has been a lot cooler in average temperature than any time in the last thirty years. The Southeast has experienced the worst drought since records have been kept with losses estimated in the billions of dollars by farmers and diarymen. This could be a taste of 'normal' weather for the immediate future in many of the southern states.

A drop in the average temperature of only a few degrees would make it impossible to grow grain in Canada and the northern tier of states in the U.S. This could be a death blow to the hungry people of the world who depend upon the bumper crops of grain from the U.S. and Canada for survival. A decrease in growing time for areas to the south of this would contribute to the shortfall and widespread climatic changes within the country could cause vegetable farmers to have substantially lower yields — sending the prices of available vegetables and fruits soaring.

The chilling of the average temperature has probably been offset somewhat by the increase in carbon dioxide in the atmosphere — creating the 'greenhouse effect.' This theory states that the increased carbon dioxide decreases the ability of the earth's surface to reflect heat back into space. The combination of these two contrary effects on the earth's climate may be likened to a house where the furnace is turned up and all of the windows opened. What the final balance in temperature will be is uncertain, but one thing is sure — the system has been tampered with and there will be disastrous results. The change in the earth's weather patterns have already begun.

Loss of the Ozone Layer

In the upper layer of the earth's atmosphere there is an extremely thin, but most important layer of ozone. This isotope of oxygen filters out a large portion of the ultraviolet radiation from the sun. Without this protective layer, life as we know it would not be possible.

Scientists have found that this ozone layer is being depleted. It is believed that chloroflourocarbons, the organic compounds used in refrigeration, aerosol sprays, and foamed plastics, are to blame for this decrease. These compounds are very much lighter than air and collect in the higher portions of the earth's atmosphere — where ozone is also found. It is believed that a chemical reaction occurs which is depleting that protective ozone layer.

A startling discovery was recently made by one of the satellites monitoring the earth's weather. This satellite found that the ozone layer over Antarctica entirely disappears during the Antarctic 'spring' which is our Northern Hemisphere's fall. The ozone layer reappears during the Antarctic 'summer,' our winter.

This hole in the protective ozone layer in Antarctica exposes an area equal in size to the United States to deadly ultraviolet radiation. If this phenomenon signals the breakdown of this barrier on a worldwide scale, it could result in the complete extinction of life on earth. Ultraviolet radiation not only causes skin cancer but may kill many of the fundamental food sources which make life in our ecosystem possible. Plankton, for instance, is very susceptible to ultraviolet radiation. So are grass and trees, which are absolutely indispensable in the cycle of carbon dioxide — oxygen regeneration on which all life on this planet depends.

Neither men nor animals could venture out of doors if there were no ozone screen to filter out this deadly radiation. Our forests would be gone, pastures incinerated, the oceans turned into stagnant cesspools of decaying fish. We have tampered with the ecosystem on which our very life depends and we will have to suffer the consequence.

But we should not be surprised at all of this; it is prophesied in the Revelation, in plain view for all to see.

The Foundations of the Earth Will Shake

Unless you live in California or another part of the world where earthquakes are common, you probably cannot even visualize what it is to have the very earth under your feet move and shake. But earthquakes are a common occurrence in the world, some 100,000 of them every year, most so minor that they are detected by only the most sensitive seismic equipment.

The earth's crust is not one continuous solid platform, but it is made up of many separate plates. These techtonic plates float on the semisolid magma of the earth's interior.

To get an idea of just how thin this solid layer of plates actually is, let us compare the earth with a peach. Consider the skin of the peach to be the earth's solid surface and the rest of the fruit to be the magma. The skin of a peach makes up 1/200th of the total mass of the peach. In contrast, the solid plates floating on top of the earth's magma make up one 1/400th of the mass of the earth. It is indeed a very thin skin on which life exists on earth.

It is believed that at some time in the past all of the earth's landmass was united in one supercontinent. But this huge mass broke up and the continents drifted apart, sometimes crashing into one another as they drifted. The land masses of today ride on these techtonic plates, but there are plates under the oceans as well.

When one plate collides with another, the heavier plate dives beneath the lighter plate. Where they grind against one another, faults occur. These fault lines are usually where major earthquakes strike.

I want to discuss one particular fault and the techtonic forces connected with it, because I feel this will have tremendous importance in the events of the end times. This is the well-known San Andreas Fault.

It is here that the Pacific plate and the North American plate meet, rubbing against each other as each moves in an opposite direction. From Baja, California, to just north of San Francisco, a portion of the edge of the North American plate has been ripped from the main body, creating this fault line. It is estimated that in about twenty million years, the pull of the Pacific plate on California will bring Los Angeles up to San Francisco.

Seismology, the study of earthquakes, is a very young science. The equipment used to measure the magnitude of an earthquake is only about one hundred years old, so that we really do not have much of an idea of how much energy can be released by one. Geologists have studied old fault lines with the adjacent movement of each side of the faults and have found some to have been enormous in the past. But we really do not know what the magnitude of the 'thousand-year quake' or the 'hundred-thousand-year quake' might actually be.

One thing most seismologists agree on, however, is that unbelievable stress has been built up in the San Andreas Fault, and someday *soon* it will be released. The size of this monster earthquake is anybody's guess.

One of the World's Greatest Natural Disasters

When the predicted earthquake strikes the West Coast, it will cause one of the worst natural disasters in recorded history. Scientists agree that this is not a matter of 'if,' but of 'when.' The San Francisco earthquake of 1906 did very little to alleviate the stress built up over possibly hundreds of thousands of years between the two techtonic plates. All that hold them from releasing this cataclysmic energy is friction. When the forces moving these plates exceed this friction factor — the largest and most-destructive natural disaster in history will occur. California, and possibly the rest of the West Coast of the United States, may cease to exist.

In the next chapter we will examine what that will mean to this country and how it all fits in with biblical prophecy. Right now we will look at something which may trigger this catastrophic event and when in the schedule of the end-times scenario it will be likely to happen.

The Earth's Wobble — Earthquake Trigger

We have seen that the earth is not a solid ball. The thin, solid crust sits atop a concentric system of semisolid-to-molten rock, iron and nickel, with a core estimated to be as high in temperature as 4,000 degrees Fahrenheit. As the earth speeds through space at about 66,000 miles per hour, it also rotates on its axis. Because it is not a solid object, the earth bulges at the equator as its revolves.

This equatorial bulge offers a larger body of attraction to gravitational forces of both the sun and the moon. These gravitational forces cause the earth to twist as it spins, producing a wobble in the earth's rotation. This causes the earth's poles to shift and, as a result, they do not always point to the same location in space.

Changes within the earth's core, coupled with the interaction of the earth's atmosphere with land, produces another wobble in the earth as it spins.

One of these wobbles has a period of one year and is called the Annual Wobble. The other has a period of 428 days and it is named after its discoverer, C.S. Chandler — the Chandler Wobble. Every seven years these wobbles are synchronized, causing the poles of the earth to zig and zag by as much as seventy-two feet.

Dr. Charles A. Whitten, chief geodesist at the National Oceanic and Atmospheric Administration, found an astonishing correlation between the seven-year wobble cycle and the occurrence of major earthquakes. In checking back through seismic records, he found that with very few exceptions, major earthquakes have occurred when the Annual and Chandler wobbles were synchronized to shake the earth the most violently.

Let us cite a few of the major earthquakes which have occurred recently during the years in which the Annual and Chandler wobbles have coincided. These include the earthquakes that occurred in Alaska in 1964, which was felt over an area of 500,000 square miles and released about twice the energy as the famous 1906 San Francisco earthquake.

In 1971 the San Fernando Valley in California experienced one that caused a billion dollars in damage. Severe earthquakes in the South Pacific, New Guinea, Turkey and Chile also occurred in 1971. In 1978 there were earthquakes in Iran which killed 25,000 people, Indonesia, and a quake in Argentina reached a magnitude of 8.2 on the Richter scale.

In 1985 two major earthquakes struck Mexico City, one at 7.8 and the other at 7.3 on the Richter scale, causing widespread damage and taking over 5,000 lives. In that same year an earthquake of magnitude 7.8 struck Chile that caused extensive damage and killed hundreds.

The Next Wobbles' Triggers

In 1992 and 1999 (recurring every seven years) the Annual Wobble and the Chandler Wobble will again be synchronized to violently shake the earth's rotation. Although the Great California Earthquake could come at any time, I believe it is most possible when the wobble forces are at their peak. Most seismologists, if forced to estimate just when this gargantuan disaster will most likely occur, agree that it could happen within the next ten to fifteen years.

11

The Fall of the United States

When the well's dry, we know the worth of water. (Benjamin Franklin)

Whenever God erects a house of prayer,
The devil always builds a chapel there,
And 'twill be found, upon examination,
The latter has the largest congregation.

(Daniel Defoe)

It seems certain that the United States will not just dismantle its nuclear arsenal unilaterally; therefore, some other cause will be responsible for eliminating this awesome retaliatory force. There are three possible explanations for this fall of the United States from its position as a superpower to being a nation under Soviet control. This nuclear deterrent could be taken out of the Soviet way by one of three scenarios: Loss of technical superiority; a preemptive Soviet first strike; or by unprecedented natural disaster. We will look at these one at a time.

Loss of Technical Superiority

Although there will be an increasing effort on the part of Congress to drastically cut military spending, I cannot foresee this as being a primary cause for the United States falling so far behind the Soviets in sophisticated weaponry as to lose completely the ability to counter a Soviet nuclear attack. The fall of the United States will not come completely from spending less on military hardware or in the research and development associated with it. The military-industrial complex just won't let that happen.

What will weaken our military power is the ever-increasing pressure from members of Congress, a vocal sector of the American public, and from our allies to reduce the threat of nuclear war by eliminating all or most of entire categories of nuclear arms. Both at summit meetings and in Soviet-American arms control negotiations in Geneva, it seems certain that additional treaties will be signed, further reducing the number of nuclear weapons on both sides. In fact, this is an absolute necessity for Gorbachev, since getting American nuclear weapons out of Europe is essential to his overall plans.

A Soviet Preemptive First Strike

Former President Richard Nixon recently stated, "We are still ahead under the sea and in the air. Our submarine-based missiles and our air-launched weapons are superior to those of the Soviet Union. But the Soviet Union is decisively ahead in the most-powerful and accurate weapons, land-based nuclear weapons. They are now able to take out the entire United States land-based missile force in a first strike, and have enough left over to take out all our great cities."

A Soviet First Strike has been in Soviet planning since 1965, when the United States first learned of it from a highly placed defector. Even had we not been given this information by a former top Soviet official, we should have been able to see what was on their minds.

Any country not intending a first strike would have, like the U.S. has done, placed its emphasis on missile-carrying submarines and not on land-based missiles. A submarine-launched ballistic missile (SLBM) is a retaliatory weapon and cannot be used ordinarily in a first strike. The reason for this is that a submarine cannot know exactly where it is with the accuracy necessary to place a missile within the 600 feet of an enemy missile silo which is built of steel-reinforced concrete. It would take a nuclear detonation that close to destroy the silo and prevent it from launching retaliatory missiles. Land-based intercontinental ballistic missiles (ICBMs) can know *exactly* where they are and the latest weapons of the United States, the Minuteman, and the Soviet SS-18, model 2 and SS-19, model 1 are thought to be capable of achieving a CEP (circular error probable) of 0.1. This means landing a warhead within 0.1 nautical miles or 200 yards.

A report in 1986 states that the Soviets have at least 200 SS-18s in place, with ten multiple reentry vehicles (MIRVs) each. This means the capability of landing 2,000 nuclear warheads on U.S. missile silos with an accuracy of 200 yards. This is First-Strike capability.

We shouldn't question Soviet intentions to use a preemptive First Strike, because of what they have told us. Sherlock Holmes once told his partner, "You see, Watson, but you do not *observe*." We have been guilty of the same thing with the Soviet Union; we have heard, but we have not paid attention.

In 1972 the Soviet Ministry of Defense published a book, *Marxist-Leninism on War and Arms,* which states, "Mass nuclear missile strikes at the armed forces of the opponent and his key economic and political objectives can determine the victory of one side and the defeat of the other at the very beginning of the war. Therefore a correct estimate of the elements of supremacy over the opponent and the ability to use them before the opponent does are the keys to winning such a war."

We read this, but we paid no attention. We saw, but we did not observe.

Another high-ranking Soviet military man, General A.S. Milovidov, said in 1974, "There is profound error and harm in the disorienting claims of bourgeois ideologies that there will be no victor in a nuclear war."

Again we heard, but we paid no attention.

The Soviets have at least 1,398 ICBMs in hardened concrete silos distributed around the Soviet Union in twenty-six known missile complexes. There may be more, but our satellites have not been able to detect them and without a launching system operational we cannot even get our most advanced KH-11 spy satellites into orbit.

Fortunately for us, the Soviet submarines have proven until recently to be major failures and only about 10 percent of the fleet of about eighty are at sea at a time. With the usual communist disregard for human life, the reactors on Soviet submarines are not adequately shielded, exposing their crews to radiation levels far above safety limits. There is a joke circulating in Soviet ports which asks how you can tell who the Soviet submariners are. The answer is: "They are the ones who have lost all their hair and glow in the dark." And that's not very far from the truth.

Another failure in Soviet submarines is that until very recently, all Soviet missiles were liquid-fueled. After many years of frustration, they have finally developed a workable solid propellent for rocket fuel. The liquid-fueled missiles were subject to almost-constant leaking, high corrosion of interior parts requiring constant maintenance, and extremely high 'out of service' time. Quarters are cramped enough on Soviet submarines, but leaking rocket fuel make conditions unbearable.

The recent development of a solid rocket fuel is of extreme importance in any Soviet plan for a preemptive first strike against the U.S. ICBM installations. Missiles fueled with a solid propellent are available for almost-instant launch. Liquid fuels, on the other hand, are quite unreliable, requiring frequent maintenance, fuel changes, and a long pre-launched checkout time. It is estimated that when the Soviet missiles were all liquid fueled, of their total of 1,398 land-based ICBMs in place, only about 980 were available at any one time for launch, with a reliability rate of only 50 percent. This means that of the total missiles fired, only 490 could be counted on to perform as expected. This leaves only a small margin for error in order in wipe out the total American long-range, land-based retaliatory missiles.

Solid fuel in Soviet missiles changes all that, and allows firing of Soviet ICBMs simultaneously to avoid 'fratricide' — the destruction of incoming warheads by previous nuclear blasts before they land on target. To avoid this, all warheads must land at exactly the same time on silos in the immediate area within blast range.

The Soviet Strategic Rocket Force consists of about 413,000 rocket troops, who are charged with the responsibility for all Soviet missiles with a range of over 1,000 kilometers (620 miles). In each Soviet missile silo there are four men on each watch. Two of these are regular servicemen specialists who handle the technical aspects of the launch. The other two are KGB soldiers who are responsible for arming the nuclear warheads. The Soviets have gone to great lengths to assure that no missile is launched without proper authority, thereby risking the start of a nuclear war by accident.

The Soviet government has in the past been afraid to allow nuclear warheads out of the Soviet Union. It is believed that the short-range missiles, bombers and artillery stationed in Eastern European Warsaw Pact nations are without nuclear ammunition. The warheads for these weapons are stored within the Soviet Union and are mated to their delivery systems only in a time of crisis or in combat-training exercises.

The authority to fire nuclear missiles or weapons rests with the Defense Council, a semi-secret body in the Kremlin. However, it is believed that Brezhnev assumed the power to order a nuclear attack himself, the reason given being that an immediate response would be necessary in case of an American preemptive nuclear attack.

Soviet practice, however, proves that they know full well that the United States will never launch a preemptive surprise attack. There is no Soviet 'black box.'

Wherever the president of the United States goes, a military officer trails behind only a few feet away. This officer carries the famous 'black box,' an electronic link between the President and the military command center where the communications are located which control the launching of American nuclear missiles in case of enemy attack.

Since there is only about a half-hour of warning between an enemy launch being detected by U.S. radar installations and the nuclear impact, not one moment can be lost by the President in ordering a counterstrike. The Soviets have complained loud and long about the danger which American nuclear missiles pose to them. Listening to the Soviets, one would believe that a warmongering U.S. President and blood-thirsty Pentagon were ready at any moment to let loose our nuclear weapons and destroy the peace-loving Soviet Union. It is the Americans, they say, who are willing to provoke a nuclear war.

But the fact that there is no 'black box' belies what they say. No Soviet officer follows the General Secretary around, carrying an electronic link with the Russian command center. In the event of an

American nuclear First Strike, the leader of the Soviet Union would be powerless to order a counterstrike by Soviet missiles.

Why?

The reason is simple. The Soviet Union and its leaders know full well that the United States will never order a nuclear attack. Our nuclear deterrent is not designed to accomplish that. The United States does not have enough land-based missiles and warheads that are sufficiently accurate to take out all of the Soviet ICBM silos. An American First Strike would fail miserably, and it would provoke a Soviet counterstrike which would destroy our country.

Why, then, are the Soviets building more and more ICBMs, more warheads, and increasing the accuracy of their weapons? There can be only one logical explanation. They are preparing for a First Strike.

The Soviet Union now has the capacity to destroy American missiles in their silos before they can even be launched against Russian targets. Their missiles are capable of destroying most of the long-range bombers of the Strategic Air Command on the ground. But a percentage of SAC bombers are always in the air. Don't the Russians fear that these intercontinental bombers will penetrate Soviet air defenses to deliver a smashing retaliatory nuclear attack?

An examination of Soviet build-up in air defense answers that question. The Soviet Union bristles with ground-to-air defenses. Antiballistic missiles ring Moscow. Gorbachev has ordered an enlargement of the underground shelters deep beneath the Kremlin that contain command posts that are impervious to nuclear destruction. These refuges are capable of housing all of the high-ranking Soviet officials, military commanders and technicians required to carry on a nuclear war. [1]

Soviet civil defense has been in place for years, while in the United States it has been considered both too expensive to maintain and too ineffective to be worthwhile. There are two Soviet civil defense organizations which operate together, the military and the civilian staffed forces. Over the years there has been a steady and gradual improvement in the efficiency of Soviet civil defense and practice alerts have been held, principally in areas of major importance. But since this civil defense system involves the evacuation of entire cities before a nuclear attack, it seems that the Soviet population as a whole would have to depend upon the effectiveness of the Soviet First Strike and the air defenses and not on any well-developed system of shelters such as the elite of Moscow have. But again, communist ideology is not opposed to the sacrifice of many of its own citizens in order to achieve its goals.

The Soviet military planners seem convinced that their ground-to-air missiles and their force of 2,600 interceptor fighters, many of which have all-weather capability, will be able to shoot down the majority of SAC bombers before they could penetrate Soviet air space.

We have not accounted for a retaliatory strike by American nuclear submarines, just one of which carries sufficient MIRV warheads to destroy every major Soviet city. It is highly possible that the Russians have already deployed satellites capable of tracking our submarines. In that event, their destruction would be rather easy using nuclear missiles.

Economic Disaster

World War II brought about the very factors which will end in the downfall of the United States as a world power. Were it not for that great war, the Soviet Union under communism would have collapsed under the weight of its own oppression, for communism produces a bankrupt society in a very short period of time. But World War II thrust the USSR into the twentieth century and endowed it with the most powerful military force in all of history. But the war did something else, and this is what will cause the fall of America to Soviet arms. World War II catapulted many underdeveloped nations into manufacturing giants, and placed them in direct competition with the industries of the United States.

At the end of World War II American money rebuilt the war-ravaged industry of western Europe and Japan and allowed the cheap-labor nations such as South Korea, Taiwan, Hong Kong and Singapore to enter the world markets once dominated by U.S.

manufacturers. Suddenly the world grew smaller, and the United States found itself in a position of competitive inferiority with the very nations whose industries we financed and built.

American industry not only finds it difficult to compete in the world market, but now is losing much of our own domestic market to the importation of foreign goods. Prior to World War II the stamp 'Made in Japan' was synonymous with poorly made goods — junk. But no more. The Japanese are now producing products which compare favorably with anything in the world.

Japanese cameras have cornered the world market. Automobiles with names like Toyota and Nissan are as common on American streets as those named Ford or Chevrolet. And their quality is as good or better.

The American automobile manufacturers have been hard-pressed to compete with imported cars, but the U.S. steel industry has found the situation utterly impossible. American steel mills are, for the most part, antiquated as compared with the modern mills in foreign nations which were built with American foreign-aid money after World War II. These foreign automated mills, coupled with the low wage rate and lesser fringe benefits paid to their labor force, has forced the closing of the majority of the U.S. steel mills. Many steel producers have declared bankruptcy and there will be more to follow. Steel, once the hallmark of the American industrial complex, is dead.

American textile manufacturers are also in trouble, with imported textiles taking a larger and larger share of the domestic market. The textile mills which moved to the South when the wage rates demanded in New England made production costs excessive, have nowhere else to look but overseas for competitive labor rates. The American textile industry is in deep trouble and no amount of 'Buy American' campaigns can save it. The automated mills and cheap labor of the foreign competition has too much of an edge.

America's jugular vein is its dependence on imported oil. The simple fact is that we cannot do without it. The U.S. economy runs on oil and no matter what the price per barrel is, we must either buy it or shut down our whole society. It is as simple as that. We are an energy-intensive nation with insufficient sources of domestic energy to sustain ourselves. And we must pay the price to foreign oil producers.

The combination of our non-competitive status in the world market with our goods and our heavy imports of foreign materials means a negative monetary flow. Each year our deficit in balance of payments — the money we owe to other nations versus what they buy from us — is increasing tremendously. The United States, for the first time in our history, has become a debtor nation.

New jobs created are by and large in service industries. These are helping to replace jobs lost in manufacturing, but do not help us in the foreign marketplace substantially. It is difficult to export services, and it is in the loss of exported manufactured goods that we find ourselves in trouble.

The Trade War

The government has attempted to persuade foreign countries to open up their domestic markets to increased American goods, but with only limited success. Japan, in particular, has been reluctant to do this. This leaves only one alternative, and this is one of the policies which will deepen America's problems in international economics —protectionist legislation.

There will come a time in the immediate future when the loss of jobs in U.S. industry will provoke Congress to pass laws establishing import restrictions on foreign goods. This, however, will cause foreign countries to retaliate with increased restrictions against American manufactured goods. Since U.S. manufacturing plants are capable of producing far in excess of goods consumed domestically, this will make the unemployment situation worse in this country instead of better. The cure in this case will cause a much more serious disease.

Uncle Sam, the Bad Guy

There is a rising anti-American sentiment in the world today. Protectionist legislation will cause a rapid and violent increase in hatred for anything American in much of the world. The Japanese and other industrialized countries will rush in to fill the void in the world market, leaving the United States in an isolated economic position.

If we were not dependent on foreign oil, this situation would be bad enough, but our absolute need of oil imports will result in an ever-increasing deficit in balance of payments. Skyrocketing oil prices will make this situation a catastrophe, with a torrent of money flowing out of the United States into foreign markets in the Middle East. Along with the negative cash flow will come a drastic increase in American interest rates —coupled with rising inflation and unemployment. But the straw that will break the camel's back in the American economy will be the default of the Third World debts owed to U.S. banks.

The Bailout, Again the U.S. Taxpayer

The United States government will have to make good on deposits insured under the Federal Deposit Insurance Corporation, putting a huge drain on the treasury and the budget. Congress will have no choice but to increase taxes to unprecedented levels. The nation will be thrown quickly into the deepest depression ever experienced, worse by far than that of the 1930s.

But America's troubles will not yet be over. In the midst of this economic disaster, we will be struck with something that this country has never before experienced. There will be catastrophic natural disasters such as the world has never seen.

Natural Disasters Strike

A natural disaster of proportions we described earlier, when the California quake occurs, could bring this country to her knees. In the course of less than a moment of time, this nation could suffer such a catastrophic blow that it might never be able to recover. Not only would we suffer in loss of life, but the economic effects of such a disaster would completely overwhelm our ability to remain a functioning state, much less a world superpower.

But the West Coast is not the only area that can experience such a devastating earthquake. Both the Midwest and the Southeast have suffered major earthquakes in the past and could very well be struck by them again. The highest-magnitude earthquake recorded in this country was at New Madrid, Missouri, in 1811. Fortunately, at that time, the area affected was only sparsely populated and little actual damage resulted, but an earthquake there today of the same magnitude would cause astronomical damage and loss of life.

On August 31, 1886, an earthquake registering 7.7 on the Richter scale struck Charleston, S.C. This quake was felt as far away as Chicago. Again, if one of this magnitude were to strike the Southeast today it would result in a significant loss of life and property over a wide area of the country. And this area is far overdue for a major earthquake. One of that magnitude has been calculated to be possible every 100 years in South Carolina and every twenty years in the Southeast.

What would happen if a major quake struck New York City? The Northeast is in fact seismically active, with minor quakes being reported regularly. The U.S. Geological Survey's *National Atlas of the United States (1970)* indicates that sometime between 1638 and 1664, New York City suffered an earthquake of VII to VIII intensity on the Modified Mercalli scale. This area, too, is long overdue for a major earthquake. Can you visualize the horrible damage and death caused by the falling of New York's skyscrapers on the streets of Manhattan? In the event of the total destruction of New York City, what could possibly take its place in the American financial system?

Earthquakes and vulcanism are closely related. The eruption of Mount St. Helens a few years ago could be a signal that something more ominous lurks just over the horizon of time. When Krakatoa erupted, or more correctly — blew up — in 1883, half the earth was darkened for six months. For a period of three years the solar radiation was reduced by about 20 percent. Temperatures in many parts of the world dropped severely and winters all over were uncommonly harsh.

When the United States sinks into the mire of depression, the entire world will be affected by it. Ours is a world economy and what happens to the American economy drastically affects the economy of the whole world. This is also in keeping with the prophecy of the end times. The nations of the earth will be experiencing great internal and external problems. Since they will be powerless to resolve these problems, they will be quite receptive to the antichrist's solution of "one world government."

12

World Conquest and
the Great Tribulation

Big Brother is watching you. (George Orwell)

The hottest places in hell are reserved for those who in time of great moral crisis maintain their neutrality. (Dante Alighieri)

The conquest of the world will begin with the First Strike to eliminate the American nuclear deterrent. This could well be preceded by a 100-megaton nuclear detonation high in space above Chicago.

Scientists have known for many years that nuclear blasts release a high-intensity electromagnetic pulse (EMP) by the interaction of gamma and X-rays with air molecules in the upper atmosphere. This high-energy radiation actually knocks electrons from the air molecules. These are called Compton Recoil Electrons. They are released at extremely high-energy levels and produce a billiard-ball effect as they collide with other molecules in the earth's atmosphere, spiraling in unison and being trapped by the earth's magnetic field. In a fraction of a microsecond they radiate like a wave from a radio-transmitting antenna.

Anything metal can pick up these electrons and where these electrons fall on wires or unshielded electronic circuits they can induce current in the order of thousands of ampheres. The wires and electronic components self-destruct. Telephone lines, power lines, computers, transistorized electronics, and even the wires in the ignition systems of automobiles are burned out by these induced high-energy currents. Anything within a visual sight line of the blast not shielded can be damaged. A blast at 250 miles up can be 'seen' in a radius of about 1,350 miles.

On July 9, 1962, a rocket carried a nuclear warhead 280 miles into the atmosphere above Johnston Atoll in the Pacific Ocean. This nuclear blast was named Starfish Prime and was calculated to be a 1.4 megaton detonation.

The resulting EMP was felt in Hawaii, some 925 miles away, where detection devices went off their scales and even street lights went out. Unfortunately this was the first and last test of its kind, for soon after the United States agreed to ban all above-ground nuclear tests.

The situation may be much worse now than then. Since that time we have seen the influx of highly sophisticated electronics and the replacement of tubes, which are more resistant to damage, with miniaturized transistors which are extremely susceptible to EMP destruction. It is somewhat ironic that the Soviets who are well behind the United States in advanced electronics and still depend greatly on tubes instead of scarce transistors are considerably less prone to the damaging effects of the EMP generated by a high-altitude nuclear blast.

I have included this explanation here because many people do not realize how vulnerable we actually are. We, as Americans, have never seen the devastation of war since none of us were around the last time. This last occurred to us during the Civil War. We cannot visualize any nation defeating the great United States of America. We certainly cannot cope with the thought that the Soviet Union will conquer the entire world — including us. Subconsciously we push any such thoughts out of our minds. We do not *want* to hear them! It can't possibly happen to us!

A single nuclear burst over Chicago would knock out all electronic and electrical equipment in a radius which extends as far east as Bermuda and Halifax, Nova Scotia; as far south as Brownsville, Texas, and Miami, Florida; as far west as Salt Lake City and Denver; and north well above our early-warning screen of radar installations in Canada. Washington, New York, Philadelphia, Atlanta, St. Louis, and all other cities, towns and rural areas would find themselves without even small transistor radios to tell them what to do in the emergency. There would be no electric power. Cars, busses, trains and planes would have their wiring burned out. Our military command centers, linked by fiber optics, would still function, but the general public would be isolated without communications, power and transportation. *Just one nuclear detonation can do this!*

The vast oceans no longer protect our shores. At any time, day or night, we are only thirty minutes away from a nuclear holocaust from Soviet-based ICBMs.

The Beginning of the Fall

I believe that sometime in the very near future we will look back and point to the date of January 28, 1986, as the beginning of the fall of the United States. With the shuttle disaster, we have begun our slide from world superpower to a state utterly devastated and broken, no longer able to defend ourselves, or the Free World, from the onslaught of the antichrist and his domination of the world.

Since the Challenger catastrophe, the United States has failed time after time to successfully launch satellites into orbit. On April 18, 1986, an Air Force Titan 34D exploded seconds after liftoff, destroying the military satellite it was carrying.

On May 3, 1986, a Delta rocket had to be destroyed by range safety officers when it went out of control shortly after liftoff from Cape Canaveral. On April 25, 1986, another rocket failed, this one a Nike-Orion, as it was launched from White Sands, New Mexico. •

Our other rockets, Titan, Delta and Atlas-Centaur — the only boosters capable of orbiting heavy payloads such as advanced military satellites and essential scientific experiments — have been grounded by these failures. We have suddenly found ourselves impotent in space.

We are powerless to stop, or unwilling to face, the ever-increasing menace of communism in South and Central America. A few years ago — thirty at the most — we would not have dreamed of tolerating such a thing. But something has sapped our national 'guts,' and we have begun the slide into a state of helpless indifference. The Roman

Empire experienced the same thing, but it took 800 years then to do
what less than a generation has done to us.

The Conquest of Western Europe

Standing between the Soviet and Warsaw Pact forces in East
Germany and Czechoslovakia is West Germany and the majority of
NATO forces are stationed there. The North German Plain is ideally
suited for tank warfare and it is this flat, open terrain where the
invasion of Western Europe will most likely begin.

With the American nuclear weapons no longer there, and the
United States in shambles, there may not be any resistance at all to the
Soviet army's entrance into Free Europe. But even if resistance is
encountered, the Soviet and Warsaw Pact forces will overwhelm it in
short order.

Defending the border of the Free World in West Germany are the
NATO forces consisting of fifteen Infantry Divisions, seven Armored
Divisions and one Airborne Division, representing the United States,
England, Belgium, Canada and the Netherlands. These units defend a
line over 600 miles in length. They are spread very thinly.

In East Germany there are ten Soviet Motorized Infantry Divisions,
ten Tank Divisions, four East German Motorized Infantry Divisions
and two East German Tank Divisions. Farther south in
Czechoslovakia, there are five Soviet Motorized Infantry Divisions
and two Tank Divisions, five Czech Motorized Infantry Divisions,
five Czech Tank Divisions and one Czech Airborne Regiment.

Right from the start, even if the Soviets moved no more troops up to
the front, the Free World is outnumbered twenty-three to forty-three
in combat divisions. But NATO has only an additional twenty-four
divisions in reserve. The Soviet Union and the Warsaw Pact can throw
an additional 114 divisions into combat in a very short time, without
even calling up reserves from trained Soviet civilians. Without nuclear
weapons, the defense of Europe is impossible. This is why it is
imperative for Gorbachev to negotiate their removal from Europe.
And without the long-range American nuclear 'umbrella,' neither
England nor France will risk using theirs for fear of Soviet nuclear
destruction of London and Paris.

The Soviet Union needs the industrial complexes of Western Europe. Gorbachev will probably get them without firing a shot, along with all of the skilled manpower to run these industries for the benefit of the new communist masters in the Kremlin.

The antichrist will issue a warning to the Western European countries to disband and disarm their military forces or face total destruction. Without the United States and its power backing them, these nations will realize it would be folly to resist. They will comply with the Soviet demand. The Red flag will fly over all of the Western European capitals.

Trained Soviet administrators will be flown into these countries to set up the new governments. Many people who will claim to have been in sympathy with Soviet aims all along will come forth. The new administrations will have no trouble finding willing hands to assist them. Any reluctance by the civilian population to obey the strict new laws will be met by harsh punishment. After a few public executions, the will of the people will be completely broken. With all hope gone, they will obey in silence. The deep black pall of doom will settle over Europe.

The Middle East

The antichrist will waste no time in occupying the Middle East. From the bases in Afghanistan, Red Army tanks will rumble through Iran toward the Persian Gulf and the Strait of Hormuz. Iraq and Syria, of course, will welcome the arrival of the Soviet Airborne divisions. The Saudis will be warned to offer no resistance. Without the U.S. military might behind them, they will have no choice. But the Soviets will stop short of attacking Israel. In spite of controlling the lands to the north and east of Israel, they will leave Israel alone for the time being. The attack on this nation will come later.

Africa

The Soviet Union has been undermining the continent of Africa for years. After World War II the European colonies in Africa became targets for a communist-inspired attack against 'imperialism.' One by one, these former colonies have gained their independence from European nations, without regard to their ability to govern themselves or to provide for the welfare of their peoples. In many of these lands, the void created by colonial administrations was filled with violence. From that violence came the establishment of Marxist-type governments in several of them, regardless of the wishes of the majority of the people of those nations.

The stabilizing force in southern Africa has been the Republic of South Africa. Regardless of what one thinks of the racial policies of that government, the South African military force has prevented Soviet influence and Marxist takeover in the entire southern portion of the continent. But that stabilizing factor will disappear in one of the most bloody uprisings in history.

The Soviet-controlled Marxist government of Mozambique has been funding and supplying the revolutionary African National Congress (ANC) for years. The ANC has operated a terrorist campaign against white farmers in rural areas of South Africa and white citizens on city streets. But there will come a time in the near future when this group will have sufficient arms to launch a general uprising among the blacks, and on sheer force of numbers they will massacre most of the 18 percent white population of South Africa.

This may occur even before the antichrist begins his world conquest. But in any event, the Soviet Union will take control of the African continent with little trouble. Bases in Mozambique, Ethiopia, Angola and Libya will provide the jumping-off points.

South and Central America

The Soviets have already achieved a toehold in the Western Hemisphere, in Cuba and Nicaragua. This will be expanded even before the fall of the United States as Nicaragua draws American troops into combat in Honduras and El Salvador. We may be able to stay out of actual combat as long as the Contra forces fight Nicaraguan troops on the Honduran border and the situation in El Salvador remains somewhat stable, but the United States certainly cannot remain only an arms supplier when Nicaraguan troops invade these countries. Marines will go in first, followed by U.S. Army and Navy involvement.

With worldwide, anti-American sentiment growing, the United States will be sharply criticized for this intervention. Even the American public will react against sending American boys to die in Central American jungles. Our Air Force will be prevented from bombing Nicaraguan cities because of the civilian casualties this would incur, leaving our infantry to slug it out with experienced Nicaraguan soldiers in the green hell of the jungle.

As soon as the United States falls, there will be many rebellions and takeovers in South and Central America by communist-backed groups. Using Cuban bases to supply them, these communist takeovers will be successful. Even the people, hard pressed by many of the right-wing military governments of today, will join in this 'War of Liberation.'

Mexico

Mexico is a powder keg ready to explode. The Institutional Revolutionary Party has been in power continually since 1929 and has become so corrupt that there is no such thing as justice for the ordinary Mexican citizen.

Mexican elections have become a farce, with ballot counting supervised by government people, insuring the election of IRP candidates. Governors of many provinces have established small 'kingdoms' of their own, financed by illegal drug traffic into the United States. Not even the federal government in Mexico City can control these powerful feudal lords.

The current government of Mexico maintains very friendly relations with both Cuba and Nicaragua. It will not take much for Mexico to declare itself with the world communist states, welcoming the world communist government which the antichrist will establish.

The Far East

The vast bulk of land and a population of one billion makes the People's Republic of China the dominant nation of the Far East. Once considered the world's greatest threat to peace, China has of late been too engrossed in its internal problems to cause trouble. But the ideology of this nation remains communist and the avowed aim of communism is world domination.

The North Korean invasion of South Korea was stopped and repelled by a determined American President and people. The attempt to stop communist aggression by North Vietnam resulted in a humiliating defeat for the United States. As a result, South Vietnam, Cambodia and Laos fell to communist control, and Thailand threatens also to go. The Vietnamese army, supplied by the Soviet Union, has become one of the world's most powerful military forces. When the United States falls, the whole of Southeast Asia will fall with it into communist hands.

The Philippines, having ousted the Marcos regime, faces increasing internal pressure from communist rebels. Here, as in Mexico, remote provinces are controlled by local 'war lords' with their own armies to protect their interests. If the current democratic government is deemed a greater threat than the communists, these provincial armies may well fight on the side of the communist insurgents against the Aquino government. When the United States falls, there will be no doubt of the outcome. The communists will control the Philippines.

The one nation capable of resisting communist aggression in the Far East has been prevented from establishing an effective military force. Japan, who once threatened the entire Pacific, has not been allowed to rearm. Although Japan's economy has been astonishing since the end of World War II, there is an active and violent communist party organization. When America falls, Japan will be unable to resist communist takeover.

The World Government Established

Advocates of "one world government" will cooperate willingly with the antichrist in its establishment. The 'New Age' movement [1] has many proponents in today's world and these people will welcome a central world government.

The antichrist will also find an already-established organization on which to base a world government. This has existed since the end of World War II in the form of the United Nations.

This world organization, despite the lofty aspirations held at its conception, has already become a forum for the communist bloc and Third World nations to vilify the United States and condemn Israel, while praising the efforts of the PLO and other radical and terrorist groups. Using funds supplied principally by the United States, it has fostered the spread of communism and the overthrow of democratic governments around the world. It has served as a base for Soviet espionage in this country while claiming diplomatic immunity for the legion of KGB and GRU agents serving on the staffs of Soviet bloc nations.

The current United Nations headquarters in New York will probably not be the site for the world government after the fall of the United States. The radioactive fallout over the northeastern U.S. will probably preclude the use of this building. But the newly organized governments of the world will certainly send delegates to some new central headquarters, possibly in the Soviet Union, and will vote in sweeping changes in the United Nations Charter, giving the antichrist absolute dictatorial powers over the member nations. The antichrist will become the supreme ruler of the world.

An Omen of Things to Come

Are there any indications that point to the United Nations being used by the antichrist as his vehicle for ruling the world?

The United Nations recently adopted a symbol of world peace and commissioned an artist to paint a mural depicting that symbol. It was painted by Elizabeth Von Janota Bzowski and hangs in the lobby of the United Nations building in New York.

It is a painting of a *white horse!*

It has the United Nations emblem at its head with colored ribbons stretching from the white horse to all the continents of the world.

In the Book of Revelation, John saw this white horse. And he saw who was riding on it. Revelation 6:2, "And I saw, and behold a white horse: and he that sat on him had a bow; and a crown was given unto him: and he went forth conquering, and to conquer."

The white horse is the symbol of the antichrist. Why did the United Nations choose the white horse as a peace symbol? The universal symbol of peace has always been a white dove. Why not the dove?

That is easy to understand. The white dove is the symbol of God's Holy Spirit. The antichrist cannot be represented by this dove. The white horse is the symbol of the antichrist. This is a portent of things to come. The United Nations will welcome the antichrist riding on his white horse of world conquest. His painting is already hanging there.

The New World Religion

When the antichrist addresses the world, every television set on the globe will be tuned in. The entire population of the world will hang upon his every word, for their fate now depends on the whims and wishes of this new world dictator. He will announce a new era in the history of mankind, a new world where all will share in the global resources, in the new advances in science and technology. This will, he claims, be an era of eternal peace and prosperity. Never again will there be war, for there will be no more national armies or national self-interests to cause it.

There will be a new religion. Mankind, he says, now controls its own destiny. Abolished are the foolish superstitions of the past. The state is now the high priest of this new religion.

Moslems will proclaim him as a reborn Mohammed. Buddhists will recognize him as the most profound in the long line of Buddhas. Hindus will place his statue in their sacred places. Other religions will do much the same. All will follow him, except devout Christians and Jews who will reject this new state religion and will suffer the consequences of their faith.

Israel, Alone in the World

The State of Israel alone will refuse to obey the orders of the antichrist. They will know that surrender would mean national suicide. The antichrist will ignore this affront. There is too much to be accomplished for him to bother with one tiny nation. But he will eventually get around to Israel at the Battle of Armageddon.

The Great Tribulation

I believe that the world is at the threshold of the period which Christ called the Great Tribulation. We are seeing today an acceleration of economic and political troubles. Famines are ravaging some areas of the world. Climatic changes are in evidence, with drought in some places and floods in others. The first signs of major and worldwide epidemics of new diseases are being experienced. All these will intensify to unprecedented proportions in the immediate future. International terrorism will increase and more democratic governments will fall to communism.

The time of the Great Tribulation is indeed upon us.

We have seen that the beast John saw rising from the sea has appeared. We have seen that he controls the mightiest military force ever assembled in history. The technology exists in place today for his conquest of the world. Satan has prepared his seat of power; the ten other kings have given him the authority and strength to accomplish his goals. The United States stands upon the very precipice of destruction. We are indeed nearly at the beginning of the Great Tribulation.

How Long?

The total length of this period of evil and sorrow is not given to us, but we are told how long after the antichrist conquers the world it will be when Jesus Christ will return and defeat this evil one and his Satanic forces.

The event we are to look for next is the healing of the 'deadly wound.' Immediately after that will come his war with the saints and the establishment of his world government and world religion. Then we are told in Revelation 13:5: "And there was given unto him a mouth speaking great things and blasphemies; and power was given unto him to continue forty and two months."

Forty-two months — three and a half years! After the antichrist has taken control of the world there will be a time of terrible persecution of Christians, and the most horrible events in all of history which will last for three-and-a-half years. This time will see the destruction of at least two-thirds of the world's population, cataclysmic natural disasters, epidemics of new and horrible diseases, great famine, and total chaos.

But you may protest that you will not have to go through this time of Great Tribulation. You may have been taught that you will be taken out of the world by the Rapture before this time of trouble and trial.

The fact is you won't be 'raptured' until after the Great Tribulation. We will deal with the question of the Rapture in our next chapter.

The Horror to Come

But now we will examine the prophecy and see just what you and I — and every human being on the face of the earth — must face when the world suffers the most intense three-and-a-half years of hardship, terror, and destruction in all of history.

We will use the Scriptures to get this picture of the Great Tribulation. Jesus said, "...For then shall be great tribulation, such as was not since the beginning of the world to this time, nor shall ever be" (Matt. 24:21).

Jesus Christ has said this is coming, but He also gives us assurance that we will not be alone. Matthew 28:20 affirms, "...lo, I am with you always, even unto the end of the world."

God assures the believing Christian that no matter what happens, He is in complete control. The Kingdom of God on earth will arrive at the end of this period of great troubles, persecution and cataclysmic disasters. In fact, many Christians do not realize that when they pray the Lord's Prayer, they are actually *asking* God to send this time of woe upon the earth, for we pray "Thy Kingdom come ..." in this prayer and God's Kingdom cannot come to earth until after this Great Tribulation period is over.

Will Christians Suffer?

This is not to say that Christians will not suffer tremendous hardship, or even death, during this time. They will, and the Revelation prophecy says so, but if God is in control of these events then nothing will be too great for the devout and dedicated Christian to bear.

John gives us a clear picture of what will come in this Great Tribulation. There will be two separate and distinct periods. The first will be the result of the antichrist's conquest of the world and the persecution of Christians after he has taken control. Christians will suffer much during this time. The second series of events, and by far the most terrifying, will come when God, himself, pours out His divine wrath upon the earth. This second series of events will come quickly, and at the very end of the three-and-a-half years of the Great Tribulation.

It should be obvious that the events John describes in his vision are not necessarily chronological. He sees two separate visions of the antichrist: the first in Chapter 6 where he is mounted upon a white horse, and the second time in Chapter 13 when he sees him rising as a beast from the sea.

Between these chapters, John's vision includes events which happened far in the past, some of them taking place possibly even before the creation of the earth. These events include the war in heaven when Lucifer, along with a third of the angels, rebelled against God's authority and were cast out. With this in mind, some of the plagues sent to earth seem to be duplicated during the opening of the Seven Seals and the sounding of the Seven Trumpets. I will make no attempt to explain this apparent overlapping of events, but just present what John sees and hears and reports to us in his book of the Revelation.

The Seven Seals Are Opened

Revelation 5:1 tells us of the Sealed Book, "And I saw in the right hand of him that sat on the throne a book written within and on the backside, sealed with seven seals."

This is God's book of judgment. It is the same book which Daniel was shown in similar vision over 600 years before John's vision. It is described in Daniel 12:9, "And he said, Go thy way Daniel: For the words are closed up and sealed until the time of the end."

Someone was needed to open the seals of this book. It must be someone who has earned the right to open the seals. John tells us of this in Revelation 4:2-3: "And I saw a strong angel proclaiming in a loud voice, Who is worthy to open the book, and loose the seals thereof? And no man in heaven, nor in earth, neither under the earth, was able to open the book, neither to look thereon."

This book was, in a sense, a legal document. It was the authority necessary to judge the world. Only one person has the right to judge mankind and to punish the world for all of the accumulated sin and disobedience since Adam fell and the world yielded to Satan's temptations and lies. Only Jesus Christ has taken on himself all of the sins of the world, every single sin of every person who ever lived, and by His sacrificial death on the cross and His victorious resurrection, has earned the right to open this Sealed Book.

John is told this in Revelation 5:5-7: "And one of the elders saith unto me, Weep not: behold the Lion of the tribe of Juda, the Root of David, hath prevailed to open the book, and to loose the seven seals thereof. And I beheld, and, lo, in the midst of the elders stood a Lamb as it had been slain, having seven horns and seven eyes, which are the seven Spirits of God sent forth into all the earth. And he came and took the book out of the right hand of him that sat upon the throne."

The Seven Seals

The first seal released the antichrist, riding on a white horse and wearing a crown and carrying a bow, riding to conquer the world. The Second Seal released the Red Horse of war, which the antichrist brings to the earth. We have already read the Scriptures concerning these first two seals and the horsemen which they release.

Famine

Revelation 6:5-6 tells of the next horseman: "And when he had opened the third seal, I heard the third beast say, Come and see. And I beheld, and lo a black horse; and he that sat on him had a pair of balances in his hand. And I heard a voice in the midst of the four beasts say, A measure of wheat for a penny, and three measures of barley for a penny; and see thou hurt not the oil and the wine."

The Black Horse means famine. It also denotes great economic problems for the world, and this actually goes hand in hand with famine.

But the Black Horse which John sees in his vision will bring a famine to the world as never seen before. There will be a real shortage of food. Climatic changes will so affect the growing of crops that even those people with money will not be able to purchase enough of it.

Economic Disaster

The world today is teetering on the verge of a great economic collapse. And there is absolutely nothing the world can do to prevent it. There are three major economic powers in the Free World today —the United States, Japan and West Germany. All three are showing definite signs of plunging into a deep recession.

A few short years ago the economy of the United States seemed to be growing at a healthy 3 percent rate. But a detailed look at this shows much cause for concern. After correcting for inflation, it was discovered that sales to consumers, business and the government were actually *falling* at an annual rate of 1.7 percent. The inflated figures reflected stockpiles of unsold inventory, not actual sales of finished goods. In this period, the value of raw materials on hand and unfinished manufactured goods rose by forty billion dollars.

At the same time it was noted that the gross national product of Japan, the second-largest world economy, was falling at a 2 percent annual rate after correcting for inflation. In West Germany, the Free World's third-largest economy, the GNP was falling at an annual rate of 4 percent.

Even with the dollar falling in value versus foreign currency, which the United States had hoped would increase the exportation of American goods, our balance-of-payments deficit is steadily increasing, because in their own declining economies Japan and West Germany do not have the increasing markets to absorb more U.S. exports.

The last four recessions in the past twenty-five years in the United States were caused by the government applying the economic brakes to stop inflation. And in each case the government used its economic powers to stop these recessions by increasing the money supply, lowering interest rates, cutting taxes and increasing government spending. None of these techniques can be successfully used today because of the enormous deficits experienced by this country. We will have to cut spending by the government, and this is already mandated by Gramm-Rudman, and increase taxes to reduce the deficit. Both of these measures will accelerate and intensify the recessionary trends.

If the Federal Reserve Board lowers interest rates, it is likely that there will be a run on the dollar which will deprive this country of the foreign money it now depends upon. If this happens, the United States might have to raise interest rates to stimulate domestic investment in U.S. bonds and notes and also print huge amounts of new money, causing the return of double-digit inflation.

We are over an economic barrel and there is absolutely nothing we can do to stave off the deep economic recession — possibly a disastrous depression — into which the world is about to plunge.

To return to the Revelation prophecy, John heard the voice say, "A measure of wheat for a penny, and three measures of barley for a penny, but hurt not the oil and the wine." Looking at what had occurred just previously in the Roman world of that time, and will also occur today, this somewhat peculiar statement makes sense.

At the end of the first century A.D., when John received this vision, the Roman Empire had experienced a drastic food shortage. Prices had risen exorbitantly for grain — the staple of the world's food then as it is today.

A penny was a day's wages for a man. With his penny he could buy one measure of wheat which would provide him with a minimum level of sustenance for one day. But a man with a family to feed would have to purchase the three measures of barley with his penny. This would enable a man, his wife and perhaps two children to live. But what about men with large families to feed?

While grain and other food items were scarce at that time in the first century, there was a plentiful supply of both olive oil and wine. This is what the voice in the background refers to when he says, "Do not hurt the oil or wine." Perhaps when the famine comes in the Great Tribulation there will be plentiful supplies of oil and luxury items, television sets, cars, boats and the like. There will certainly be a plentiful supply of wine and whiskey. The comment made by the voice in the background of John's vision may be very appropriate to our time.

Pestilence

The Fourth Seal released another horse. Revelation 6:8: "And I looked, and behold a pale horse: and his name that sat upon him was Death, and Hell followed with him. And power was given unto them over the fourth part of the earth, to kill with the sword, and with hunger, and with death, and with the beasts of the earth."

The Pale Horse is the aftermath of war and disaster. He brings disease along with his companions, War and Famine. There will be epidemics such as have never before ravaged the earth. And we are told that a fourth of the earth's population will perish. That is more than *one billion people!*

The world will be in desperation, in economic chaos, with raging epidemics and widespread famine. The antichrist will proclaim that he has the solution to the world's problems. And he will be hailed as the savior of the world.

But what about Christians? Will they have to face this? Won't God take them out of the world before this horror strikes? What about the Rapture?

I believe that the opening of the Fifth Seal reveals the answers to these questions, which will be dealt with in detail in the next chapter.

Death

Revelation 6:9: "And when he had opened the fifth seal, I saw under the altar the souls of them that were slain for the word of God, and for the testimony which they held."

Here John is shown the souls of Christians who had been killed in the first part of the Great Tribulation. No, these are not — as some Rapture proponents claim — the souls of Christians who have been martyred over the past 2,000 years. The Scriptures that follow show exactly who these people are.

Revelation 6:10: "And they cried out with a loud voice, saying, How long, O Lord, holy and true, dost thou not judge and avenge our blood on them that dwell on the earth?"

These martyred souls are crying out to God to avenge them. But many more Christians are still alive on earth, still in the Great Tribulation.

Revelation 6:11 gives them their answer: "And white robes were given unto every one of them; and it was said unto them, that they should rest yet for a little season, until their fellow-servants also and their brethren, that should be killed as they were, should be fulfilled."

This Scripture gives us great insight into the Rapture question. These were the first martyrs of the Great Tribulation, but more Christians were yet to be killed.

These martyrs of the Great Tribulation had been greatly honored, for to be buried under the altar is indeed a great honor bestowed by God. But there remained on earth many more who were also to suffer martyrdom before the Lord would avenge them all by pouring out His wrath upon the earth. These martyrs were given white robes and told to rest until everything in God's plan had been completed pertaining to the Christians yet to give their lives for their testimony for Jesus Christ.

God knows even the number of hairs upon each of our heads. He also knows the exact number of Christians living today who are willing to be killed, to suffer martyrdom for their faith. Until every last one of these is killed by the antichrist and his evil forces, the avenging cannot occur.

Natural Disasters

The Sixth Seal is described in Revelation 6:12: "And I beheld when he had opened the sixth seal, and, lo, There was a great earthquake; and the sun became black as sackcloth of hair, and the moon became as blood...."

Natural disasters will strike the earth; the first one will be an earthquake that will raise such a huge quantity of dirt and dust into the earth's atmosphere that it will blot out the sun. The moon at night will be seen as blood-red through the darkening of this atmospheric contamination.

The earthquake described here will be of enormous intensity, and perhaps this is the one which will destroy the West Coast of the United States, for we are told in Revelation 6:13-14, "And the stars of heaven fell unto the earth, even as a fig tree casteth her untimely figs, when she is shaken by a mighty wind. And the heavens departed as a scroll when it is rolled together; and every mountain and island were moved out of their places."

This sounds as though the earth is being bombarded by meteors, or perhaps the great earthquake is accompanied by tremendous volcanic activity — volcanic explosions which send fiery bursts of molten rock high into the air, looking like falling stars. This earthquake will indeed be tremendous, for we are told that it will move mountains and islands. This will cause great panic on earth.

Revelation 6:15-17 tells us: "And the kings of the earth, and the great men, and the rich men, and the chief captains, and the mighty men, and every bondman and every free man, hid themselves in the dens and in the rocks of the mountains; And said unto the mountains and rocks, Fall on us, and hide us from the face of him that sitteth on the throne, and from the wrath of the Lamb: For the great day of his wrath is come; and who shall be able to stand?"

It sounds from this that many people on the earth will realize what is happening, that the wrath of God is causing these great natural disasters. They will know that they are reaping the results of their sins. Nothing like this has ever happened before, at least not since the flood in which only Noah and his family survived. They know that they cannot hide from the wrath of God.

But when this happens will all Christians be gone from the earth? Will they have all been martyred? No. The next verses show that there will still be Christians on the earth during this terrible time.

Christians Are Sealed

Revelation 7:2-3 states, "And I saw another angel ascending from the east, having the seal of the living God: and he cried out with a loud voice to the four angels, to whom it was given to hurt the earth and the sea, Saying, Hurt not the earth, neither the sea, nor the trees, till we have sealed the servants of our God in their foreheads."

It is perfectly evident that Christians will remain on earth in the midst of all of these terrible events. In Revelation 7:4-8 we find that 144,000 are to be sealed with the Seal of God, 12,000 from each of the twelve tribes of Israel. But these cannot be Jews, for these 144,000 all have the testimony of Jesus Christ. In theomatics, the number 144 stands for salvation. I believe that the 144,000 refers to all the Christians who will be remaining on earth at this time.

The tribes of Israel cannot be found today. Ten tribes were taken captive into the Assyrian Empire and were absorbed into that culture and lost forever. Judah and Benjamin were taken captive to Babylon. Many intermarried with Babylonians and they were not a pure Hebrew culture when they returned. I believe that the 144,000 represents the *spiritual* children of Abraham, for we are told by Paul in Galatians 3:28-29: "There is neither Jew nor Greek, there is neither bond nor free, there is neither male nor female: for ye are all one in Christ Jesus. And if ye be Christ's, then are ye Abraham's seed, and heirs according to that promise."

All Christians who are bond-servants to God will be sealed in their foreheads with the Seal of God by the angel. But many, many Christians will have died or will have been martyred during this part of the Great Tribulation. John sees these people in Revelation 7:9-10: "After this I beheld, and, lo, a great multitude, which no man could number, of all nations, and kindreds, and people, and tongues, stood before the throne, and before the Lamb, clothed in white robes, and palms in their hands; And cried with a loud voice, saying, Salvation to our God which sitteth upon the throne, and to the Lamb."

Who are these people? Why do they carry palm branches? We get the answers to these questions in Revelation 7:13-14: "And one of the elders answered, saying unto me, What are these which are arrayed in white robes? And whence came they? And I said to him, Sir, thou knowest. And he said unto me, These are they which came out of great tribulation, and have washed their robes, and made them white in the blood of the Lamb."

This multitude of people are not raptured Christians. These people have suffered. They have been through at least a part of the Great Tribulation. This is made clear by what the elder tells John in the verses of Revelation 7:16-17, "They shall hunger no more, neither thirst any more; neither shall the sun light on them, nor any heat. For the Lamb which is in the midst of the throne shall feed them, and shall lead them unto the living fountains of waters: and God shall wipe away all tears from their eyes."

These people will not be raptured out of the world before the Great Tribulation, before the antichrist conquers the world, before disaster strikes the earth. They will experience famine, feel the sun's strong rays and the intense heat which is described among the plagues which smite the earth during the tribulation. They will know great sorrow. But God will wipe away all their tears and the Lamb will feed them and give them His living water. These people will suffer greatly, but their suffering will come to an end, when they are safe in the hands of God for all eternity.

A multitude of people, far too many for a man to count, will die during the Great Tribulation. They will be different from the Christian martyrs. These people will have perished in the war, from famine and from the earthquakes, floods and other natural disasters which will strike the earth. These will be ordinary people, little people who went about their lives unnoticed by the world, but who carried the salvation of Jesus Christ in their hearts. They will not be heroes as the martyrs are, but people from all walks of life, from all nations, from all tongues and races of the earth who have believed in Jesus Christ and have lived according to God's simple laws of behavior. But their reward is eternal life under God's protection and care. They are the 'meek' which shall inherit the earth when Jesus Christ returns to establish God's Kingdom.

The Seventh Seal Opened — The Beginning of God's Wrath

Revelation 8:1, "And when he had opened the seventh seal, there was silence in heaven about the space of half an hour."

Silence in heaven!

Something awesome was about to happen!

Revelation 8:2 tells us: "And I saw the seven angels which stood before God; and to them were given seven trumpets."

The Seven Trumpets

The seven trumpets usher in another phase of the Great Tribulation on the earth. God will now begin to avenge those who have suffered at the hands of the antichrist, the false prophet, and their master — Satan.

In Revelation 8:3-6 we read: "And another angel came and stood at the altar, having a golden censer; and there was given to him much incense, that he should offer it with the prayers of all saints upon the golden altar which was before the throne. And the smoke of the incense, which came with the prayers of the saints, ascended up before God out of the angel's hand. And the angel took the censer, and filled it with fire of the altar, and cast it into the earth: and there were voices, and thunderings, and lightnings, and an earthquake."

The prayers of the saints who will be martyred will reach God, mingled with the smoke of the incense. Now God will avenge them.

God Avenges His Martyrs

The First Trumpet is described in Revelation 8:7: "The first angel sounded, and there followed hail and fire, mingled with blood, and they were cast upon the earth: and the third part of trees was burnt up, and all green grass was burnt up."

The nuclear war in which the antichrist will destroy the American nuclear deterrent and enable him to conquer the world and the great natural disasters, such as huge earthquakes, will so drastically change the earth's weather pattern that storms will develop in gigantic proportions. The clouds of dust and dirt which will obscure the sun and moon will plunge temperatures around the globe. Hail of unprecedented size and quantity will be produced by enormous storms which will punish the earth with massive bolts of lightning, setting afire vast areas of forests and grasslands.

Hail is formed when rain is carried high up into the atmosphere by updrafts within the centers of low pressure. The frigid air condenses the water droplets and as long as the updraft is sufficiently strong to keep the weight of the ice particles suspended, they grow larger and larger as more water condenses on them. The longer they are in the upper atmosphere, the larger they become. Finally, when their weight is too much for the suspending currents, they drop to earth as hail. Many storms will produce hail as large as softballs.

Hail is one of the most destructive elements in storms, because it is capable of leveling entire fields of crops, smashing windows, and injuring people who are caught unprotected. These super storms described in John's vision could be accompanied by hurricane-force winds and violent tornadoes. Such weather conditions would be deadly, and that is exactly what John is describing.

God used a similar storm to punish the Egyptians when Pharaoh refused to let the Israelites go. This is described in Exodus 9:24-25: "So there was hail, and fire mingled with the hail, very grievous, such as there was none like it in all the land of Egypt since it became a nation. And the hail smote throughout all the land of Egypt all that was in the field, both man and beast; and the hail smote every herb of the field, and brake every tree of the field."

This is the type of storm John saw, except that it was very much larger and much more powerful. This was followed quickly by another plague on the unbelievers on the earth. Revelation 8:8-9 states: "And the second angel sounded, and as it were a great mountain burning with fire was cast into the sea: and the third part of the sea became blood; and the third part of the creatures which were in the sea, and had life, died; and the third part of the ships were destroyed."

Wormwood

This is a description of widespread destruction, with over a billion people of the earth killed, a third of the trees, the grass, and now the sea and all the creatures in it, as well as the ships, have been destroyed. The next trumpet brings more devastation on the earth as we are told in Revelation 8:10-11: "And the third angel sounded, and there fell a great star from heaven burning as it were a lamp, and it fell upon the third part of the rivers, and upon the fountains of waters; and the name of the star is called Wormwood: and many men died of the waters, because they were made bitter."

The burning mountain and the burning star which will fall into the ocean and into the fresh water of the earth could be meteorites, but I believe this may describe something else. A hydrogen bomb utilizes the same enormous energy source as a star, hydrogen fusion. What these verses may be describing is the fallout of the nuclear detonations which the antichrist will use to eliminate the American nuclear deterrent.

The majority of these nuclear missiles would strike the North Central section of the United States, principally North Dakota, Nebraska, Idaho and Montana. The fallout from these nuclear detonations would be mainly in an area of about 300 miles downwind, or eastward, from these points. But not all of the fallout would be confined to North America. The effects would be evident all over the earth. In the case of the Soviet nuclear power plant accident in 1986, the radioactive fallout affected areas as far northwest as Norway and Finland, rendering reindeer meat so dangerous that this may have totally destroyed the way of life for the Laplanders who depend almost exclusively on the reindeer for survival.

The Great Lakes represent the largest body of fresh water in the world. They are in the direct path of radioactive fallout from the North Central states. The contamination of these lakes would result in the loss of a third of the world's fresh water.

As the Great Lakes drain into the North Atlantic Ocean, the radioactive contamination would eventually poison this great sea as well. All of the events John sees in his vision as pertaining to the plagues and catastrophes which strike the earth in the Great Tribulation may be explained in the light of twentieth-century technology, when man became capable of destroying the very planet on which his survival depends.

Another cause of the death of the oceans may be from the debris from nuclear explosions and earthquakes and volcanic activity which would prevent adequate sunlight from reaching the seas. This would be disastrous to plankton, the first link in the marine food chain. Fish which depend on plankton for food would die quickly.

Even without the diminished effect of solar radiation, an atomic war could seriously affect the ozone layer of the earth's atmosphere, which is even now being diminished by aerosol use, allowing massive amounts of ultraviolet radiation to reach the earth. This, too, would destroy the plankton in the world's oceans, since plankton grows very near the surface of the water. Either one or both of these situations would seriously effect the earth's biosystem and could even destroy one of the world's most important sources of food, the oceans and seas.

The Sun Darkened

John heard the Fourth Trumpet sound in Revelation 8:12: "And the fourth angel sounded, and the third part of the sun was smitten, and the third part of the moon, and the third part of the stars; so as the third part of them was darkened, and the day shone not for a third part of it, and the night likewise."

This sounds exactly like the conditions which would exist during what scientists have called a 'nuclear winter.' So much debris, dirt, dust, soot and smoke will be blown into the earth's atmosphere that only a portion of the natural sunlight will be able to penetrate it. This follows exactly the pattern of the death of the oceans which we just examined in the last section. The terrible aftermath of nuclear war will inflict horror on the earth and all its inhabitants.

Revelation 8:13 tells us: "And I beheld, and heard an angel flying through the midst of heaven, saying with a loud voice, Woe, woe, woe, to the inhabiters of the earth by reason of the other voices of the trumpets of the three angels, which are yet to sound!"

The Plague of Stinging Locusts

The Fifth Trumpet is described in Revelation 9:1-3: "And the fifth angel sounded, and I saw a star fall from heaven unto the earth: and to him was given the key to the bottomless pit. And he opened the bottomless pit; and there arose a smoke out of the pit, as the smoke of a great furnace; and the sun and the air were darkened by reason of the smoke of the pit. And there came out of the smoke locusts upon the earth: and unto them was given power, as the scorpions of the earth have power."

The earth will be scourged by swarms of stinging insects, having venom as powerful as a scorpion. Contrary to popular belief, the sting of most species of scorpions is not fatal, although it is extremely painful. Locusts, as these insects are described, feed on vegetation. But not these insects. They have only one victim in mind — man. But God will not allow them to harm Christians.

Then follows Revelation 9:4-5: "And it was commanded them that they should not hurt the grass of the earth, neither any green thing, neither any tree; but only those men which have not the seal of God in their foreheads. And to them was given that they not kill them, but that they should be tormented five months: and their torment was as the torment of a scorpion, when he striketh a man."

This horde of stinging insects, as numerous as a plague of locusts, infests the earth for five months, which is exactly the life-span of a locust. Men dare not venture out of doors for fear of them. Could this be an insect which has been changed or mutated by radioactivity? Certainly man's experiments with genetic engineering could open a 'bottomless pit' of genetic monsters upon the world.

The sting of these insects causes excruciating pain, for we are told in Revelation 9:6 what men will seek to relieve this pain: "And in those days men shall seek death, and shall not find it; and shall desire to die, and death shall flee from them."

God's wrath will not be cheated, even by death. For five months those who have not the seal of God in their foreheads will be tormented. They will experience a foretaste of the torment that they will receive for all of eternity after the Second Resurrection when they will be cast into the lake burning with unquenchable fire.

One woe is past, and the second woe comes. The Sixth Trumpet sounds in Revelation 9:13-15: "And the sixth angel sounded, and I heard a voice from the four horns of the golden altar which is before

God, Saying to the sixth angel which had the trumpet, Loose the four angels which are bound in the great river Euphrates. And the four angels were loosed, which prepared for an hour, and a day, and a month, and a year, for to slay the third part of men."

War Between Russia and China?

These four angels do not kill men themselves. They open the door for what appears to be a huge army to do battle. We read about this in Revelation 9:16-18: "And the number of the army of the horsemen were two hundred thousand thousand: and I heard the number of them. And thus I saw the horses in the vision, of them that sat on them, having breastplates of fire, and of jacinth, and brimstone: and the heads of the horses were as the heads of lions; and out of their mouths issued fire and smoke and brimstone. By these three was the third part of men killed, by the fire, and by the smoke, and by the brimstone, which issued out of their mouths."

Two hundred thousand thousand! An army of 200 million men! There is only one nation on earth capable of fielding such an army —Red China. What these verses indicate is that there will be a war between the Soviet Union and Red China for control of the world. During this war a third of the world's population will be killed. When this total is added to what Revelation has told us previously, it means that by this time in the Great Tribulation over half of the people on earth will have been killed.

This war is not the final battle which will be fought at Armageddon. This war, probably between the two communist superpowers, will be fought sometime before the final Battle of Armageddon. I believe that the reference to the time the angels have been preparing for this may give us a clue as to when in the timetable of the end times this war is fought. The thirteen months of preparation may signify that this war will come thirteen months after the antichrist has taken control of the world.

The Unrepentant Earth

Even with all of these plagues, wars, famines, epidemics and economic disasters, men will apparently not learn anything. We are told as much in Revelation 9:20-21: "And the rest of the men who were not killed by these plagues yet repented not the works of their hands, that they should worship devils, and idols of gold, and silver, and brass, and stone, and of wood: which neither can see, nor hear, nor walk: Neither repented they of their murders, nor of their sorceries, nor of their fornication, nor their thefts."

By this time Satan will have so infiltrated the men of the earth that even with all of this evidence of God's power, many will still refuse to repent and turn to Him.

By this time it seems possible that all Christians will be dead with the exception of the 144,000 who have been sealed in their foreheads with the seal of God. With this exception, only the decadent, perverse and evil will remain on the earth. It is upon these that God will pour out an even-greater measure of His wrath.

The Wrath of God Poured Out

The sounding of the Seventh Trumpet is delayed, for when this last trumpet sounds, *there will be no more time.* At the sounding of this final trumpet, Jesus Christ will return to earth in power and glory. "For the Lord himself shall descend from heaven with a shout, with the voice of the archangel, and with the trump of God: and the dead in Christ shall rise first: Then we which are alive and remain shall be caught up together with them in the clouds, to meet the Lord in the air: and so shall we ever be with the Lord" (1 Thess. 4:16-17). We are told more about this in Revelation 10:7: "But in the days of the voice of the seventh angel, when he shall begin to sound, the mystery of God should be finished, as he hath declared to his servants the prophets."

God has delayed the sounding of the Seventh Trumpet so that His wrath might be poured out from the Seven Vials, or Bowls, upon the evil of the world. Revelation 15:5-7 tells us: "And after that I looked, and behold, the temple of the tabernacle of the testimony in heaven was opened: And the seven angels came out of the temple, having the seven plagues, clothed in pure and white linen, and having their breasts girded with golden girdles. And one of the four beasts gave unto the seven angels seven golden vials full of the wrath of God, who liveth forever and ever."

At this time a third of the land and a third of the sea will have been destroyed. Two-thirds of the world's population will have been killed, either by war, famine, natural disasters, or disease. A horde of insects with the sting of a scorpion will have ravaged them for five months. Most of the drinking water will have been poisoned by radioactive fallout. The sun and moon will have been dimmed by the dense clouds of debris and dust in the atmosphere, causing a nuclear winter. All over the earth men will fight among themselves, blaming each other for what is happening. The armed forces of the antichrist are using the most brutal and inhuman methods to try to maintain a semblance of order.

Then the earth will experience something far worse, even more terrible than what has previously occurred. God will pour out upon the earth His wrath, undiluted, from the cup of His indignation. The blood of the martyrs of the Great Tribulation will be avenged.

The First Vial

The First Vial is described in Revelation 16:1-2: "And I heard a great voice out of the temple saying to the seven angels, Go your ways, and pour out the vials of the wrath of God upon the earth. And the first went, and poured out his vial upon the earth; and there fell a noisome and grievous sore upon the men which had the mark of the beast, and upon them which worshipped his image."

Those on earth who had received the mark of the beast or had worshiped his image were stricken with horrible sores on their bodies. Radiation can cause such sores, or burns. The skin peels and the open sores do not heal. There is a constant drainage of a foul discharge from the lesions.

There could be another cause for these sores. Suppose that in the act of receiving the beast's mark, these people had been tattooed with needles which had not been properly sterilized. By this time millions in the world will be carrying the AIDS virus. They will have been infected with this virus by contaminated needles in many cases.

One of the common diseases which people who suffer from Acquired Immune Deficiency Syndrome develop is a form of skin cancer (Karposi's Sarcoma) which causes multiple lesions all over their bodies. But whether these sores will be caused by radiation, AIDS or some other agent, those who have accepted the mark of the beast or have worshiped the image of the antichrist will suffer these horrible sores.

The Second Vial

The Second Vial is poured out in Revelation 16:3: "And the second angel poured out his vial upon the sea; and it became as the blood of a dead man; and every living soul died in the sea."

All the oceans are dead! We are told they are like a dead man's blood. They may even be colored red, for there are certain types of marine organisms which do not have chlorophyll but other compounds. Some of these cause the organisms to be red. They are responsible for the so called 'red tides' which kill all of the fish and other marine life trapped by them. Perhaps the oceans are now so changed that only these red killer organisms can survive in them. But whatever the cause, the oceans will become sewerage ponds, devoid of useful life.

The Third Vial

The third vial is poured out: "And the third angel poured out his vial upon the rivers and fountains of waters; and they became blood" (Rev. 16.4). Now God has poured out his plagues upon the world's fresh water.

The Fourth Vial

The Fourth Vial is discussed in Revelation 16:8-9: "And the fourth angel poured out his vial upon the sun; and power was given unto him to scorch men with fire. And men were scorched with great heat, and blasphemed the name of God, which hath power over these plagues: and they repented not to give him the glory."

Nuclear radiation and the nuclear winter will so reduce the ozone layer in the upper atmosphere that ultraviolet radiation will create havoc on the earth. No one will be able to venture outside for more than a few moments at a time because their skin will burn and blister from exposure to the full fury of the sun's ultraviolet spectrum. Skin cancers will be widespread. Animals unprotected in the fields will be killed. Any person or animal whose eyes are unprotected will be blinded by cornea damage.

Trees such as conifers, which are essential to the world's ecosystem, will die as will an estimated one-fifth of the earth's species of plants. The remaining green vegetation will suffer reduced photosynthesis, thus reducing the amount of oxygen they release. Earth's environment will be drastically altered.

There may also be huge solar flares which would bathe the earth with increased radiation and heat. This may also be a foretaste of what the earth's evil population has to look forward to in their eternity in the lake of unquenchable fire.

The Fifth Vial

Revelation 16:10-11 tells of the Fifth Vial: "And the fifth angel poured out his vial upon the seat of the beast; and his kingdom was full of darkness; and they gnawed their tonques for pain, And blasphemed the God of heaven because of their pains and sores, and repented not of their deeds."

If Gorbachev is truly the antichrist, then the Soviet Union will be singled out for a special dose of the undiluted wrath of God. We are getting very close to this point in the end of time. In fact, the angels are now preparing for the climax, which is the Battle of Armageddon.

The Sixth Vial

The Sixth Vial is described in Revelation 16:12: "And the sixth angel poured out his vial upon the great river Euphrates; and the water thereof was dried up, that the way of the kings of the east might be prepared."

The stage is being set for the final battle. The kings of the east would seem to be the Chinese, Japanese, Vietnamese and Indians. In fact, there are reports that the Chinese have now completed a paved road leading through the mountain passes to the border of India. In any event, the 'kings of the east' will participate in the world's last battle — at Armageddon in Israel.

Revelation 16:13-14 goes on: "And I saw three unclean spirits like frogs come out of the mouth of the beast, and out of the mouth of the False Prophet. For they are the spirits of devils, working miracles, which go forth unto the kings of the earth and of the whole world, to gather them to the battle of that great day of God Almighty."

And Revelation 16:16 tells us exactly where that will take place, "And he gathered them together into a place called in the Hebrew tongue Armageddon."

The Seventh Vial

All is now ready for the climax and the Second Coming of the Lord Jesus Christ. Revelation 16:17 tells us: "And the seventh angel poured out his vial into the air; and there came a great voice out of the temple of heaven, from the throne, saying, IT IS DONE!"

The voice from the throne is God's voice. The same voice which spoke the universe into existence now calls for time to end.

The man who was born into the poverty of a humble carpenter's home, who lived a sinless life, who was killed upon a cross on a hill named Golgotha outside the walls of Jerusalem, and who defeated Satan by being resurrected from the dead will now return in glory and majesty to claim the prize He won on the cross. It is now time for the Second Coming of Jesus Christ, the Son of the living God.

God's Purpose in the Great Tribulation

Several questions arise concerning the Great Tribulation which should be answered. The first concerns the reason why God finds it necessary to put the earth and its population through such suffering, death and destruction.

Once before God chose to cleanse the earth of people who did not obey His laws and lived in sin and corruption. Only Noah and his family were saved from destruction to give the world a fresh start. It was not long after, however, that mankind reverted back to sinful ways. The reason was that Satan was still free to influence man. He was still the 'god of this world,' as Jesus called him. As long as Satan is loose on the earth, man will continue to fall victim to his lies and will reject God. But this time, after the Great Tribulation, it will be entirely different. Jesus Christ will return to rule the world and Satan will be bound for 1,000 years.

When Jesus returns to begin the Kingdom of God on earth, what do you think He will want to start with? Would He want a world full of sin and perversion with which to build a new, bright-and-shining, God-controlled world? No, I think not. The Great Tribulation will rid the earth of the trash and vileness of today's earthly population. Sin and immorality will be wiped from the face of this planet, allowing Christ's people, His saints, to start a new society completely obedient to God's will and without the influence of Satan.

Those of us who lead comfortable lives today cannot possibly comprehend what conditions will be like during this cleansing period of the Great Tribulation. We have been conditioned to expect life to go on more or less as it always has. We expect to live to see our children grow up, marry, and have our grandchildren. Mentally, we are in no way prepared to face the decisions and hardships which will confront us when the worldwide disasters strike. We will have to face the loss of our families, our jobs, our security, and even our lives.

Most people today, even Christians, are not prepared to deal with life under a hostile government. We *know* about this thing called the 'mark of the beast,' but we cannot fully realize the enormity of the decision we will be forced to make — acceptance or refusal of this mark. Nor are we able to fully understand the consequences of this decision.

The Great Tribulation will begin with something entirely alien to our thinking — the devastation of the United States by natural disaster and/or a nuclear holocaust. This is so horrible to contemplate that we blot it completely from our minds. But it is coming!

The fall of the United States from being a world superpower, with a powerful nuclear deterrent, to an impotent and helpless mass of confused and disoriented people *must* happen in order for God's plan to be accomplished. The American nuclear deterrent *has to be taken out of the way* for Gorbachev, if he is indeed the antichrist, to succeed in what John's Revelation tells us will occur — complete and total domination of the world by a Satan-led force.

Very few of us have missed more than one meal in our lives. We have lived in a land of plenty. What we have seen on our television screens in Ethiopia is absolutely foreign to us. We are firmly convinced that such conditions will never — can never — happen to us here.

But they will!

We have seen the ravages of the earthquakes which struck Mexico City from the comfort of our living rooms. We have watched devastating natural disasters from afar. But soon many of us will experience natural disasters a thousand times worse than these, with no relief agencies to come to our rescue, no Red Cross workers to find us shelter, no food to feed us. We will be entirely on our own.

When the great epidemics strike the world there will not be enough doctors, sufficient medicine, and there will be too few hospitals. Because we have not even remotely experienced anything this horrible, we cannot imagine what it will be like. But we *will* experience this, and much more during the time of the Great Tribulation. God says we will.

So far in history every prophecy made in the Bible has come to pass except the end-time prophecies.

Whenever God's prophets have foretold an event, it has happened. The only prophecy yet unfulfilled is the end-times prophecy. This, too, shall come to pass.

But Why Do Christians Have to Go Through It?

It is impossible to produce pure gold or silver without consigning it to the furnace. There, in the crucible of intense heat and flame, the impurities are purged from the precious metals. Without subjecting the ore to the fire, the metal is worthless.

The Christian must also be refined to be of use to Christ in the establishment of His Kingdom on earth. But unfortunately many will not pass this test. Zechariah told us this in writing about the holocaust of the end times. Read Zechariah 13:9: "And I will bring the third part through the fire, and will refine them as silver is refined, and will try them as gold is tried: they shall call on my name, and I will hear them: I will say, It is my people: and they shall say, The Lord is my God."

From this prophecy in Zechariah it appears that two-thirds of the Christians in the world will not pass God's test of fire in the crucible of the Great Tribulation. Only a third of Christians will be able to withstand the onslaught of Satan's fury and remain faithful to God. But to those who pass this test, this trial of faith, will be given the crown of all God's promises throughout all eternity. Nothing, absolutely nothing, can compare with that reward.

But, you may say, I have been told that I won't have to go through the Great Tribulation. I have been taught that Christ will come and take all Christians out of the world before this time of sorrows begins!

I'm sorry. That's not what the Scriptures say. Christians *will* have to go through the Great Tribulation.

13

The Rapture Question

It takes two to speak the truth — one to speak, and another to hear.
(Thoreau)

Each is given a bag of tools,
A shapeless mass and a book of rules;
And each must make, ere life is flown,
A stumblingblock, or a steppingstone.

(R. L. Sharpe)

Certainly, I wish the doctrine of the pre-tribulation rapture were true. I do not look forward to going through the horrors of the Great Tribulation or seeing my family and friends go through it. I would like very much to be 'raptured' before these unprecedented, world-wide events begin.

But *I* won't be.

My family won't be.

You won't be.

There are several variations of the Rapture doctrine. Some teach that before the Great Tribulation begins — even before the antichrist appears on the world scene — Jesus Christ will make a secret visit to earth and take all Christians back to heaven with Him. Others teach that this will happen sometime during the Great Tribulation; some teach that only some, and not all Christians will be 'raptured.' But regardless of which of these variations is believed, all who teach the pre-tribulation rapture expect the Lord to return in secret for them before the Second Coming and before God's wrath is poured out upon the earth.

"Pre-tribulation rapture" means that this will take place *before* the Great Tribulation.

"Mid-tribulation rapture" means it will take place *during* the Great Tribulation.

"Post-tribulation rapture" means it will happen *after* the Great Tribulation.

"Post-millennial rapture" means that it will occur after the thousand-year reign of Christ.

"Partial rapture" means that not every Christian will be caught up.

My Understanding of the Event Called the Rapture

What I believe concerning what the Scriptures teach about the 'rapture' is found in the events of Revelation 20:4-6. The Seventh Trumpet, the 'last' trumpet which announces the end of time, sounds as Christ and His heavenly armies descend to earth. The dead in Christ rise, those Christians living are changed; they are given 'resurrection bodies.' This is the First Resurrection. The armies of the antichrist are destroyed. The antichrist and the false prophet are seized and cast into the Lake of Fire. Satan is bound for a thousand years. The Millenium begins and Christians will reign with Christ for a thousand years.

The unjust dead will not be resurrected until the Second Resurrection at the end of the Millenium, where they will face judgment at the Great White Throne. Those of the Second Resurrection, those whose names are not found in the Lamb's Book of Life, will join Satan, the antichrist and the false prophet in the Lake of Fire for eternity.

The type of rapture teaching I want to particularly address is the pre-tribulation rapture doctrine because this is the most prominent today — and the most dangerous. Those who hold to this teaching are not at all concerned with the Great Tribulation because they are convinced that they will not have to go through it.

Those who do not expect to go through the Great Tribulation will be totally unprepared to face what it will bring. Because they are suddenly faced with something horrible that their pastor or teacher taught that they would never see, their faith *may be totally destroyed.* They could lose their salvation because of this false teaching and the shock of finding themselves in a situation they are not prepared to face.

No one ever heard of the rapture teaching before 1830. Nothing concerning a 'rapture' is contained in the Book of Revelation, which is where it certainly should be if something of that nature were going to happen in the end time.

But despite this, the pre-tribulation rapture doctrine is widely taught today. It is an absolute doctrine in some church denominations.

How, then, if it is not found in the Scriptures, was totally unknown by the early church, was not known by *anyone* until 1830, and John makes no mention of it in Revelation — did it become so widely accepted and taught today?

The Origin of the Pre-Tribulation Rapture Teaching

The early 1800s were a time of great revival for the Christian Church. This awakening touched many countries. It produced some of the most outstanding preachers and evangelists ever known. Scotland and England were in the midst of this revival and religious fervor was at a high pitch. Religious meetings were being held everywhere and were attended by large crowds.

In the small town of Port Glasgow, Scotland, a fifteen-year-old girl by the name of Margaret MacDonald had a dream. In this dream she related how she saw *some* Christians being taken bodily out of the world just before the tribulation struck the earth. This dream occurred in April of 1830.

At the same time in London, a Presbyterian minister named Edward Irving was pastoring a church. He had translated a book by a Roman Catholic priest named Manuel de Lacunza called *The Coming of Messiah in Glory and Majesty,* which the author had published in Spanish under the pseudonym, Juan Ben-Ezra. In translating this book, Irving was introduced to futurist pre-millennialism. He was greatly influenced by what Lacunza's book said, although it mentioned nothing concerning a pre-tribulation rapture. That would come from little Margaret MacDonald and her dream.

Sometime in 1831 word reached Irving that a revival had begun in western Scotland. It is not known whether Irving himself went to Port Glasgow at this time or not, but his church sent a delegation to determine just what was happening. What they brought back was both the revival and Margaret MacDonald's dream of believers being taken bodily out of the world before the onslaught of the tribulation.

Irving's church on Regent street became the talk of London, much to the dismay of the church's board of trustees. They filed a complaint against Irving and he was subsequently found guilty of violating Presbyterian order in a trial held on April 26, 1832. On Sunday, May 6, 1832, Irving and his followers were locked out of the Regent Street church. They moved to a building on Gray's Inn Road and formed what they called the Catholic Apostolic Church, with Irving as pastor.

Although Edward Irving died only a few years later, in 1834, the doctrine of the pre-tribulation rapture was launched and it began to spread. The concept was taken up by John Nelson Darby who founded the Plymouth Brethren and wrote extensively on this and other subjects. Darby visited the United States on many occasions and the Plymouth Brethren church was established on this side of the Atlantic as well, along with the doctrine and teaching of the pre-tribulation rapture.

The influence Margaret MacDonald had on this is revealed in a book written by Robert Norton in 1861 entitled, *The Restoration of Apostles and Prophets; In the Catholic Apostolic Church*. Norton lived for a time at Greenoch, Scotland, only a few miles from the MacDonalds in Port Glasgow. He knew the entire family well and was a frequent visitor in their home.

Only about eight copies of Norton's book are still in existence and had it not been for another circumstance, the idea of a pre-tribulation rapture might have quietly died. But another man read about this concept and he was to have a profound effect on its promulgation.

The Scofield Reference Bible and Notes

In his book, *The Origin of the Pre-Tribulation Rapture Teaching*, John L. Bray writes the following: "Cyrus I. Scofield (1843-1921), a

successful lawyer, educated in Tennessee, converted in 1879 while in
jail in St. Louis on charges of forgery, ordained three years later as
minister of a Congregational church, with no theological training,
became for a number of years a student of the writings of J.N. Darby.
The views held by J.N. Darby on the Pre-Tribulation Rapture became
part of the Scofield Reference Bible notes in 1909."

Scofield read Darby's books and was consequently introduced to
the idea of a pre-tribulation rapture. In 1891 Scofield attended a Bible
conference at Seacliff, Long Island, and it was there that he decided to
write what would be known as the Scofield Reference Bible. This also
included notes for additional study, and in these notes he explained the
concept of the pre-tribulation rapture. The Scofield Bible was first
published in 1909.

This idea suddenly became church doctrine in some denominations.
Some seminaries picked it up and ran with it. Other schools followed.
Soon the view held by only a handful of people became, with
absolutely no scriptural backing, a doctrine which must be believed in
a large number of churches.

All pre-tribulation rapturists point to one verse of Scripture as proof
of this concept. This Scripture is contained in Paul's first letter to the
church at Thessalonica. I think it helps to understand this verse if we
look at the historical aspect of this letter and explain just why it had to
be quickly followed by Paul's second letter to this church.

Paul and Silas had come down from Philippi, where they had
established the very first church on the continent of Europe. Paul had a
relative who lived at Thessalonica by the name of Jason, and it was in
Jason's home that a church was established. But Paul's preaching met
with immediate opposition from the Jews of Thessalonica and the
Jewish leaders instigated a plot to get rid of him. They convinced a city
magistrate that Paul's preaching would cause a riot in the city.

The magistrate imposed what amounted to a 'peace bond' on Jason
and other property holders who attended the church in Jason's home.
Under this, if any disturbance broke out because of Paul, these men
would forfeit their property. Paul knew that the Jewish leaders would
make certain that a disturbance would occur. He had no choice;

he would have to leave the city before this happened or his friends would lose all they had.

Reluctantly Paul and Silas left Thessalonica, knowing that they had only given this new church a rudimentary knowledge of Christianity and had not the time to adequately train a leader. He doubted that this church would last long, especially in such a hostile environment. He traveled south, looking for any opportunity to establish additional churches.

A few months later a passing traveler told him that the church at Thessalonica was not only still in existence but it was growing. Paul wrote them a letter of encouragement and another traveler took it north for him to the Thessalonian church.

We know this letter by the name of First Thessalonians and in chapter 4, verses 15-17, Paul wrote the following: "For we say unto you by word of the Lord, that we which are alive and remain unto the coming of the Lord, shall not prevent them which are asleep. For the Lord himself shall descend from heaven with a shout, with the voice of the archangel, and the trump of God: and the dead in Christ shall rise first: Then we which are alive and remain shall be caught up together with them in the clouds, to meet the Lord in the air: and so shall we ever be with the Lord."

Now these words written by Paul are very much in agreement with what John saw in his vision of the Second Coming of Christ after the Battle of Armageddon. But this is *after* the Great Tribulation, after the Christians in the world have experienced the hardships of it and many of them — in fact *most* of them — have been killed during it.

It is this passage which supposedly confirms the pre-tribulation rapture teaching. Even back in Paul's time it was misunderstood, for Paul received a report back from Thessalonica which disturbed him greatly. They had misinterpreted this same passage of his first letter and thought Paul was telling them that Jesus was coming back *immediately* for them, or at least very soon. They had quit their jobs, sold their property, and were sitting on top of a hill *waiting for the return of Jesus Christ!*

The reason Paul had included this passage in his letter was to answer a question they had asked him while he was still with them, but had not had time to do before his sudden departure. It concerned Christians who had died; what would happen to them when Christ did return?

Paul quickly wrote them another letter, advising them to get back to work. Many things had to be fulfilled before Christ would return. In this second letter, Paul specifically tells them that Christ cannot return until *after* the antichrist arises in the world, *after* there is a great falling away from faith, and *after* Satan sent them a lie which many would believe: "Let no man deceive you by any means: for that day shall not come, except there be a falling away first, and that man of sin be revealed, the son of perdition" (2 Thess. 2:3-12).

This part of the passage alone should convince pre-tribulationists that the antichrist *must* be revealed in the world before Jesus can return. But the rapture teaching being preached today states that the Christian Church will be taken out of the world *before* the antichrist is revealed. Paul continues, "Who opposeth and exalteth himself above all that is called God, or that is worshipped; so that he as God sitteth in the temple of God, shewing himself that he is God. Remember ye not, that, when I was yet with you, I told you these things?"

Paul asked the Thessalonians whether they remembered that he had told them what had to come before the Lord could again return to earth. Of course, he had been with them such a short time, and had tried to cram as much teaching as possible into them before he had to leave. But he had told them, and apparently they had forgotten. He continues, "And now ye know what withholdeth that he might be revealed in his time. For the mystery of iniquity doth already work: Only he who now letteth will let, until he is taken out of the way."

In this Scripture from the King James Version, we find a word which has entirely *reversed* its meaning sometime between 1611 A.D. to the present. The word *let* or *letteth,* at the time of the King James translation, meant to *prevent* or to *hinder.* Paul is telling them that the antichrist cannot come into the world until God allows him to come, and that it will be in God's timing — not Satan's. He continues, "And then shall that Wicked be revealed, whom the Lord shall consume with the spirit of his mouth, and shall destroy with the brightness of his coming. Even him, whose coming is after the working of Satan with all power and signs and lying wonders."

As we shall see when we examine what will happen at the Battle of Armageddon, Paul is telling the Thessalonians *just exactly* how Jesus Christ will destroy the antichrist and his army. Paul has certainly been given precisely the same picture of the workings of the antichrist as John would later, for he talks of the counterfeit signs and wonders which the antichrist will perform in the end times to deceive the world. He continues by telling them just why many will be deceived, "And with all deceivableness of unrighteousness in them that perish; because they receive not the love of the truth, that they might be saved. And for this cause God shall send them a strong delusion, that they should believe a lie: That they all might be damned who believe not the truth, but had pleasure in unrighteousness."

Paul gives the Thessalonians — and us — the same graphic picture of the state of the world as John does in Revelation. Since God's Word is consistent and cannot contradict itself, both Paul and John state that Christ cannot come back until the antichrist has been revealed in the world. This happens during the Great Tribulation, and since John records the words of God to the martyrs buried under the altar that their brethren must also die as they did, it cannot be denied by anyone that *Christians must go through the Great Tribulation.*

I know personally several men who are twentieth-century apostles. These men risk their lives by traveling behind the Iron Curtain to visit and minister to the underground churches. They bring back stories of modern martyrs, similar to those related by the early church father Eusebius.

In some of these countries to own a Bible is against the law and can bring a five-year prison sentence. To profess your faith in Christ can mean the same prison term. But those behind the Iron Curtain risk their lives and beg for Bibles. They go on serving their Lord under conditions you and I cannot possibly understand.

But one thing stands out in my mind from what these brave evangelists tell me. Behind the Iron Curtain, the most asked question is, "When did the Great Tribulation begin?" To them it is not a question of whether they will be raptured before the Tribulation. These people believe they are already living in the Great Tribulation.

The Christians of the early church knew nothing of the Pre-tribulation rapture teaching. They had not been taught about it nor had they heard anything about it. It was fostered by Edward Irving, J. N. Darby, and Robert Norton. This teaching was picked up by Cyrus Scofield and was included in his notes in the *Scofield Reference Bible*. It has been kept alive by certain theological seminaries and popular Christian books.

The proponents of the pre-tribulation rapture try to tell us that all through the ages Christians have been taught to believe in a secret visit by Jesus Christ before the appearance of the antichrist and before the beginning of the Great Tribulation. At that time all Christians would be whisked away, into the clouds to meet Him, along with the resurrected Christian dead.

The fact that early Christians *did not believe this* may be substantiated by reading what Irenaeus wrote near the beginning of the third century A.D. This is contained in the book, *The Ante-Nicene Fathers* [2], "For all these and other words were unquestionably spoken in reference to the resurrection of the just, which takes place after the coming of antichrist, and the destruction of all nations under his rule."

From this it is quite evident that early Christians had no such beliefs as the proponents of the pre-tribulation rapture would have us believe. The early church believed, and this is confirmed by their writings, that the resurrection of the dead in Christ would come after the antichrist had been defeated in the Battle of Armageddon. This is exactly what John tells us will happen in Revelation. There is absolutely no mention of what the pre-tribulation rapturists teach about either the living or the dead being taken out of the world before that time.

The Danger of the Pre-Tribulation Rapture Teaching

In his excellent book, *The Incredible Cover-up* [3], Dave MacPherson writes the following, "The Pre-Trib rapture view has caused the deaths of thousands of persons. Veteran missionary H. A. Baker shares his experiences of thirty-four years on the mission field in China in several books, including *Through Tribulation, Tribulation to Glory, Visions Beyond the Veil,* and *God in Ka Do Land.* He graphically points out the link between beliefs and actions.

"Baker and other post-trib missionaries warned many Chinese Christians that Antichrist would come before Christ returns. Many heeded the warning and, before the Communist takeover, fled to the mountains where they have been able to continue witnessing for many years.

"On the other hand, many pre-trib missionaries assured the believers that they would be raptured away *before* any time of persecution — and history tells us that thousands of Chinese Christians have been murdered since 1949!

"In his book *Re-entry*, page 124, John Wesley White quotes *Time* magazine as reporting that tens of thousands of Christians are now languishing in prisons in China and Russia and other Communist countries. These believers are, in some cases, undergoing torture, and their children are taken from them if they teach them about Christ.

"Corrie ten Boom has also spoken of the Chinese Christians and their suffering: 'The Christians were told that they didn't have to go through tribulation and we all know how it is in China.' She added that Christians in free lands had better prepare for what is coming to them also. And in her article, 'The Coming Tribulation' in the Nov.-Dec., 1974 *Logos Journal* she wrote that those teaching there will be no tribulation and that Christians will be able to escape all this are really the false teachers Jesus was warning us to expect in the latter days."

I want to heartily recommend another book, *Christians Will Go Through the Tribulation* [4], by Jim McKeever. This book deals with just what Christians can expect when the Great Tribulation comes and tells them how to prepare for it.

The Christians behind the Iron and Bamboo Curtains are trying to tell us to get ready for what is coming. They know first-hand what it will be like *because they are already suffering from it.* Those who teach the pre-tribulation rapture are telling us to ignore these warnings.

We have very little time left. Start now to get yourself ready. Start now by increasing your faith to withstand and resist the antichrist and the forces of evil which he will bring upon us. Try to convince those around you who have swallowed the teaching of the pre-tribulation rapture how wrong this teaching really is. You may save their lives by it.

I want to state emphatically that many of those who teach the pre-tribulation doctrine love God as much as anyone else. They are in no way conscious agents of untruth or false teachings. They are, for the most part, God-fearing and devoted Christians who sincerely believe in what they teach. But they have been taught incorrectly and are simply repeating what they have been taught by men whom they deeply respect.

The pre-tribulation rapture doctrine is very appealing. Those who initially accepted it and were responsible for its promulgation saw in the pre-tribulation rapture something that they would do — *if they were God*. Certainly, they reasoned, God *will not* make Christians go through such horror.

We are told in Isaiah 55:8: "For my thoughts are not your thoughts, neither are your ways my ways, saith the Lord."

God *tells* us in His Word that we will have to go through the furnace of the Great Tribulation in order to be refined and tried. It is not what we would choose, but it is what God has chosen.

We must accept what God has in store for us and, like Job, say, "Though He slay me, yet will I trust Him..." (Job 13:15).

14

The Battle of Armageddon

I shall tell you a great secret, my friend. Do not wait for the last judgment — it takes place every day. (Albert Camus)

Even the average man, who does not know what to do with his life, wants another one which will last forever. (Anatole France)

After some three and a half years of Satan controlling the world through his agents on earth, the antichrist and the false prophet, we will approach the Battle of Armageddon where the forces of evil will meet the Force, and the Source, of everything that is good and pure and clean and righteous — the returning Jesus Christ.

Satan has always hated the Jews. He hates them because God chose them as the agents through which He revealed himself to the world. The Jews were chosen to bear His Son who would defeat Satan and reconcile the world to God. Throughout history Satan has tried to exterminate the Jews, and attempts to accomplish this Satanic goal have accelerated in recent history.

It was certainly Satan who instilled such hatred in Adolf Hitler's mind, and in those who took part in his attempt to solve 'the Jewish problem.' He did not succeed in exterminating the Jewish people, but he did kill over eight million of them in his death camps before the end of World War II.

Satan has also placed the hatred of the Jews in the minds of many Moslems. Islamic Jihad does not have to look very hard too find millions of willing fanatics who are bent on wiping out the state of Israel, and all Jews, from the face of the earth.

The Two Planes of Existence

At this point I must introduce a concept which explains why all of the events prophesied in the book of Revelation *must* come to pass on earth. It also explains the origin of Satan's hatred of Jews, and his hatred of Jesus Christ and all Christians. This may be very difficult for many to accept and understand, but it is at the heart of all that this book is about.

The first principle is that there are two planes of existence: the physical, in which you and I are now a part; and the spiritual, which is the realm of God, the angels, and Satan. Heaven and hell are the boundaries of this spiritual world.

The Physical and Spiritual Worlds

The second principle is: whatever occurs in the spiritual world has a counterpart in the physical world. But these events do not have to happen simultaneously, although the happening always occurs first in the spiritual plane.

The Book of Revelation gives us a picture of the war between Satan and God, between good and evil, which *has already been fought in heaven.* The battle of Armageddon will be the culmination of this war, and will result in a combination of the two separate planes into one. The spiritual and physical realms will be united with the return of Jesus Christ to earth. This will be evident when we examine the kingdom set up after the Battle of Armageddon and the citizens of that kingdom.

The War in Heaven

We must first realize that our reckoning of time and God's reckoning of time are not the same. Psalm 90:4 tells us, "For a thousand years in thy sight are but as yesterday when it is past, and as a watch in the night."

With that in mind, and recognizing that John's vision is cloaked with symbolism, let us examine John's description of this war waged in heaven with the physical manifestations of it on earth.

Revelation 12:1-2 tells us, "And there appeared a great wonder in heaven, a woman clothed with the sun, and the moon under her feet, and upon her head a crown of twelve stars: And she being with child cried, travailing in birth, and pained to be delivered."

This woman, I believe, represents Israel which God chose to bring forth Jesus Christ into the world. She was clothed with the brightness of the sun, this being the knowledge of the true God which she possessed in an otherwise spiritually dark world.

Lucifer had already begun his rebellion against God and had convinced one-third of the angels to join him.

Satan could see God's plan to redeem the world and knew that the woman posed a serious threat. He was determined to destroy the Christ as soon as the woman, Israel, delivered her child.

The Red Dragon, Satan

Revelation 12:3-4 shows us this: "And there appeared another wonder in heaven; and behold a great red dragon, having seven heads, and ten horns, and seven crowns upon his heads, And his tail drew the third part of the stars of heaven, and did cast them to the earth: and the dragon stood before the woman which was ready to be delivered, for to devour her child as soon as it was born."

Stars are often used in the Bible to represent angels. The stars which the dragon's tail drew are the angels which sided with Lucifer against God. Satan, the red dragon, tried to destroy Christ, the child born of the woman, as soon as He was born. And we read of Herod and his attempt to kill the infant Jesus who had been born a new king of the Jews. This was the work of Satan, controlling the mind of the evil Herod and putting the fear of this child into his imagination as a threat to his own kingdom.

The Birth of Christ

Revelation 12:5-6 continues: "And she brought forth a man child, who was to rule all nations with a rod of iron: and her child was caught up unto God, and to his throne. And the woman fled into the wilderness, where she hath a place prepared of God, that they should feed her there a thousand two hundred and threescore days."

Mary, who symbolizes Israel, brings forth her child, Jesus, who is destined to rule all nations. The rod with which Christ will rule them is mentioned in Psalm 2:9: "Thou shall break them with a rod of iron; thou shall dash them into pieces like a potter's vessel."

An angel warned Joseph that Herod sought to kill the child and he took Mary and the infant Jesus and fled into the wilderness of Egypt.

We do not know how long they stayed there, but even after Herod's death in 4 BC there was danger, for Herod's son Archelaus who inherited Judaea, Samaria and Idumaea from his father was found to be as cruel as Herod. John would have known just how long Joseph, Mary and Jesus were forced to hide in Egypt, for at His death Jesus gave Mary's care over to John. This could be the three-and-a-half years mentioned here when the woman who had borne the man-child was hidden in a place prepared by God for her.

Another of Herod's sons, Antipas, was given Galilee and Peraea and he later proved to be a weak man, allowing his wife to trick him into beheading John the Baptist. But in any event, Joseph would not have brought his family back to Nazareth until all danger had passed and this must have been a period of several years.

Satan Cast Out of Heaven

Revelation 12:7-8: "And there was war in heaven: Michael and his angels fought against the dragon; and the dragon fought and his angels, And prevailed not; neither was their place found any more in heaven."

Here again we must realize that time as we think of it is not the same as God's time. I believe what we are reading here is the victory which Christ achieved over Satan at the cross on earth which defeated Satan also in heaven. We know that Christ's sacrificial death and His resurrection were responsible for Satan's defeat, but this was already achieved from the very beginning of time. This is illustrated by the verse in Revelation 13:8 which states," ...the Lamb slain from the foundation of the world."

We all know that Jesus, the Lamb, was not physically slain until He died on the cross, but in God's time this had already been accomplished from the first instant of the creation of the world.

In God's concept of time, this defeat was something which *had already been accomplished*, whether or not that particular event had transpired *in our limited concept of time.*

We are also told here something which is quite contrary to what Christians are usually taught. Satan no longer is given access to the throne of God. His place, we are told here, is no longer found in heaven. We know from the Book of Job that Satan stood before God and could communicate with Him. Satan convinced God to test Job's faith and loyalty, and we are all familiar with what happened as a result. But this was long before the cross, before Jesus' ultimate and final sacrifice. In Job's time, the world lived under the Law. But after Calvary and Jesus' victory, the world has been under God's grace which was bought by the blood of Jesus.

That Satan no longer stands before God's throne to bring his accusations against us is shown by the next verses: "And the great dragon was cast out, that old serpent, called the Devil, and Satan, which deceiveth the whole world: he was cast out into the earth, and his angels were cast out with him. And I heard a loud voice saying in heaven, now is come salvation, and strength, and the kingdom of our God, and the power of his Christ: for the accuser of our brethren is cast down, which accused them before God day and night" (Rev. 12:9,10).

Before Jesus Christ died on the cross and arose again in victory over Satan, the devil was free to come and go between heaven and earth. He could stand before the throne of God and not only tempt men but accuse them of falling victim to his temptations. But no longer. Now he must remain on earth, no longer to have access to the throne, no more to bring his lies and accusations against men to the Father.

But the earth is warned of what is to come: "And they overcame him by the blood of the Lamb, and by the word of their testimony; and they loved not their lives unto the death. Therefore rejoice, ye heavens, and ye that dwell in them. Woe to the inhabiters of the earth and of the sea! For the devil is come down unto you, having great wrath, because he knoweth that he hath but a short time."

In our time scale this happened less than 2,000 years ago, after Christ physically defeated Satan by His death and resurrection. But it had happened at a different time according to God's time. This is shown by what Jesus said in Luke 10:18: "...I beheld Satan as lightning fall from heaven."

Jesus said this before the cross, before He had defeated Satan. But in God's scheme of things, it was a *fact already accomplished.*

Satan now knew he had but a short time. Since he could no longer have any opportunity to defeat Christ, he turned his attention and his vengeance against the woman who had brought Christ into the physical world.

Satan's Hatred of the Jews

Revelation 12:13 tells us: "And when the dragon saw that he was cast into the earth, he persecuted the woman which brought forth the man child."

Satan hates the Jews for being the people God chose to bring forth the only person capable of defeating him. Thirty-seven years after the crucifixion and resurrection — and Satan's defeat — he tried to destroy them by using the Roman legions to wipe Jerusalem from the face of the earth. In 70 AD Titus totally destroyed this city, which also fulfilled the prophecy Jesus made when he wept over Jerusalem.

Jews from all over Palestine had fled to Jerusalem to escape the ravages of the Roman legions, who had been given the order to kill all Jews —men, women and children — they found. It has been estimated that over 1,200,000 Jews were within the walls of the city when Titus sealed it off. At the end of the siege, when the city and its defenses finally collapsed, less than 50,000 Jews had survived, and most of these were either shipped to Rome for the arena's slaughter or sold into slavery to build the canal at Corinth.

For almost 2,000 years the Jewish people would have no homeland, being scattered among all the nations of the world. Satan has tried many times since to destroy this remnant. Massacres during the Middle Ages, pogroms in Russia, and the latest attempt in Hitler's death camps. But as God promised, He saved enough of them to bring them back again to inhabit the land which He had promised to Abraham and his seed as an inheritance.

The following verses refer to these attempts of Satan to wipe out the Jewish people before God could bring them back again as a nation: "And the serpent cast out of his mouth water as a flood after the woman, that he might cause her to be carried away of the flood. And the earth helped the woman, and the earth opened her mouth, and swallowed up the flood which the dragon cast out of his mouth (Rev. 12:15, 16).

The Jews were so dispersed that Satan's efforts to eradicate them were unsuccessful. But now his anger turned to another group of people. In Revelation 12:17 we read: "And the dragon was wroth with the woman, and went to make war with the remnant of her seed, which keep the commandments of God, and have the testimony of Jesus Christ."

Satan's Hatred of Christians, Abraham's Seed by Adoption

John was a Jew as were the majority of the earliest Christians. He would naturally think of himself and those like him as being the seed of the woman, Israel. But by this time the Gentiles were becoming an increasingly large factor in Christianity, due primarily to the work of Paul. These, too, lay claim to being the seed of the woman, for we are told in Galatians 3:29: "And if ye be Christ's, then ye are Abraham's seed, and heirs according to the promise."

The wrath which Satan has against both Jews and Christians has been in evidence since the days of Nero, Domitian, Trajan and most of the Roman emperors up to Constantine, who himself became a Christian in 313 AD, and established Christianity as the state religion.

But Satan did not forget his wrath nor let up in his attempts to destroy both Christians and Jews. He has been busy setting up counterfeit religions to draw men away from their faith in the true God. He threw the Mongol hordes against the Christian countries of Europe, then the armies of Islam, which almost succeeded in the seventeenth century when Moslems occupied an empire extending from Egypt to the Caspian Sea and northward almost to Vienna, and half of Spain.

Within our own lifetimes we have seen Satan inspire the madmen of Germany and Japan to try to conquer the world and impose Satanic totalitarian governments upon all mankind.

Then, out of the defeat of Nazi Germany, came the rise of yet another Satanic empire, one which will now succeed in Satan's plans for ruling the world. The Soviet Union, with the most powerful military force ever assembled, embued with Satan's atheistic lies, is now led by the man who fulfills all of the Revelation prophecy of the antichrist.

The world, according to man's reckoning, has reached the end times. Satan's fury is now raging. The final act in God's plan is being played out on the world stage. Most of the characters are already in place.

The final battle is shaping up at Armageddon. The curtain of time is about to draw across the world. Jesus Christ is ready to return to earth — this time not as the son of a poor carpenter from Nazareth — but in power and glory and majesty.

The Kingdom of God is at hand!

The Final Battle — Armageddon

All of Satan's frustration in not being able to destroy the seed of the woman, Israel — both Jew and Christian — will be unleashed by the antichrist upon the small nation which still remains free. Over the rest of the world all men will do his bidding. School children will chant his name, adults will worship his image and bear his mark on their foreheads or hands. From most buildings huge photographs and paintings of him will hang. Only Israel will remain defiant.

This tiny nation will become "a festering sore" for Satan and the antichrist. Surrounded on all sides by hostile forces, she will manage to avoid being swept up in the world conquest by the Soviet and Warsaw Pact armies. But Israel's time will come. The antichrist will remove this stumbling block in his way of total domination of the earth.

Around the year 500 BC, Zechariah prophesied about this very time. He wrote, "And in that day will I make Jerusalem a burdensome stone for all people: all that burden themselves with it shall be cut in pieces, though all of the people of the earth be gathered together against it" (Zech. 12:3).

And in that day, the antichrist will indeed summon all of the armies left in the world against this small piece of land, Israel and its capital, Jerusalem.

The antichrist will summon the armies of the world together against Israel. John describes this in Revelation 16:13-14: "And I saw three unclean spirits like frogs come out of the mouth of the dragon, and out of the mouth of the beast, and out of the mouth of the false prophet. For they are the spirits of devils, working miracles, which go forth unto the kings of the earth and of the whole world, to gather them to the battle of that great day of God Almighty" (Rev. 16:13, 14).

The Place of the Final Battle

And Revelation 16:16 tells us where this will take place: "And he gathered them together in a place called in the Hebrew tongue Armageddon."

This site of the final battle is a pass leading to the Plain of Esdraelon. It is mentioned in the ancient tablets found at Tell-el-Amarna and written about 1400 BC. It was captured by the Egyptian Pharaoh Thotmes in 1483 BC. Ancient Assyrian inscriptions mention this place. It is where King Josiah was slain and where Solomon built great stables for his horses.

This place is only about fifteen miles from the city of Nazareth. When Christ returns to earth to do battle here, He will be, in a sense, "coming home," this time to stay.

Over 2,500 years ago God gave his prophet Ezekiel a vision of this last great battle and those who would participate in it. Reading the thirty-eighth chapter of his book is like reading the front pages of today's newspaper. We can see the world's events shaping up exactly as God said they would over 2,500 years ago.

The Antichrist's Armies

"Son of man, set thy face against Gog, the land of Magog, the chief prince of Meshech and Tubal, and prophecy against him, and say, Thus saith the Lord God; Behold, I am against thee, O Gog, the chief prince of Meshech and Tubal: And I will turn thee back, and put hooks into thy jaws, and I will bring thee forth, and all thine army, horses and horsemen, all of them clothed with all sorts of armor, even a great company with bucklers and shields, all of them handling swords. Persia, Ethiopia, and Libya with them; all of them with shield and helmet: Gomer, and all his bands; the house of Togarmah of the north quarters, and all his bands: and many people with thee" (Ezek. 38:2-6).

Persia, which is present-day Iran and Iraq; Ethiopia, now a Marxist state allied with the Soviet Union; Libya under the lunatic Khadafy —all of these were named over 2,500 years ago and here they are at Israel's throat today. The other nations, Gog and Magog and Meshech: these names of Noah's descendants have been identified by Josephus [1] as originating the people of Scythia, who later migrated north to populate what we know now as Russia.

Gomer was said by Josephus to have founded the Galacians in what we now know as Turkey, and the Gauls who migrated northward and may be the ancestors of the Germanic people. All of these will be represented in the army of the antichrist when he leads them against the last stronghold of opposition on the face of the earth — the State of Israel.

Israel Stands Alone

The Israelis will have to stand alone. There will be no aid from the United States, which will have been reduced to less than a third-rate nation. There will be no help coming from European nations, now under the control of the antichrist. Israel will stand alone against the mightiest military power ever assembled in history, and with the knowledge that defeat will mean total and complete annihilation.

Israel will have only one hope. God had promised to send them a Messiah in their day of despair. But they have already received their Messiah and rejected Him. They allowed him to be killed, crucified by the Romans at the instigation of their religious leaders. They failed to recognize Him when He came! Is there any hope for them now?

Yes! He is coming again! This time He will come in power and glory. This time they will see Him for what He is: the Son of the Living God, their Messiah!

The Israeli Army Crushed

With all of the might of the antichrist's armies against her, Israel will still not call on the Lord to save her. The Israeli government will still rely on the Israeli military forces to defend the land against overwhelming odds. Although the Israeli army and air force will fight valiantly, they will prove to be no match for the superior numbers of the forces of the antichrist. After a heroic stand, they will be decimated. The antichrist's armies will overrun Israel and occupy Jerusalem.

We are told about this in Zechariah 14:2: "For I will gather all nations against Jerusalem to battle; and the city shall be taken, and the houses rifled, and the women ravished; and half the city shall go forth into captivity, and the rest of the people shall not be cut off from the city."

The antichrist will himself triumphantly enter Jerusalem. With Israel defeated, the whole world is now at his feet. Satan rules the entire earth. Now the antichrist, as the agent of Satan, can stand on the holiest place on the face of the earth and proclaim himself master of it all, the god-ruler of the whole world.

Satan has at last realized his ambition. He rules the world through his agents, the antichrist and the false prophet. He is worshiped along with them as a god.

But Satan's victory will be short-lived.

God Enters the Battle

"And it shall come to pass in that day, that I will seek to destroy all the nations that come against Jerusalem. And I will pour out upon the house of David, and upon the inhabitants of Jerusalem, the spirit of grace and of supplications: and they shall look upon me whom they have pierced, and they shall mourn for him as one mourneth for his only son ..." (Zech. 12:9, 10).

Now God is ready to take a hand in the matter, for His people have called out to Him for help. But the cost has been great for Israel. Two-thirds of the Israelis will die before the people will humble themselves and call out to God to help them.

Now the stage is set for the return of Jesus Christ. All that must happen first has now happened, and heaven prepares for that great event. The Seventh Trumpet, which has remained silent up till now, is about to sound —and there will be *no more time.*

Christ Makes Ready for Battle

Just as John saw the antichrist as a conqueror riding upon a white horse, he now sees the King of kings and Lord of lords seated upon a great white horse, ready to do battle with the antichrist and his armies. Revelation 19:11-13 tells us what he saw: "And I saw heaven opened, and behold a white horse; and he that sat upon him was called Faithful and True, and in righteousness he doth judge and make war. His eyes were as a flame of fire, and on his head were many crowns; and he had a name written, that no man knew, but he himself. And he was clothed with a vesture dipped in blood: and his name is called The Word of God."

The Return of Jesus Christ

The first coming of Jesus as a babe born in a lowly manger went for the most part unnoticed by the world. But the Second Coming will be quite different. This time all those left on earth will see Him coming in majesty and glory and power in the clouds. His army of the heavenly host will be following Him as He descends upon the Mount of Olives just outside the city of Jerusalem.

Can you imagine the astonishment of the soldiers of the army of the antichrist as they see this magnificent heavenly host descending? Can you picture the look on the faces of the antichrist and the false prophet? Total panic will seize these evil men as they realize that their day of victory has turned suddenly into total and everlasting defeat.

John's book of Revelation tells us few details about the Battle of Armageddon. But the other Old Testament prophets do. Zechariah 14:4 tells us the exact point on which Christ's feet will touch the ground. "And his feet shall stand that day upon the Mount of Olives, which is before Jerusalem on the east, and the Mount of Olives shall cleave in the midst thereof toward the east and toward the west, and there shall be a great valley; and half the mountain shall move toward the north, and half of it toward the south."

As Jesus' feet touch the earth there will be a great earthquake which will split the Mount of Olives. His armies will follow Him and we get a picture of them in Revelation 19:14: "And the armies which were in heaven followed him upon white horses, clothed in fine linen, white and clean."

Israel's Messiah Returns

Can you picture the thrill of the remnant of Israel as they witness the coming of their Messiah to rescue them from total destruction at the hands of the antichrist? But they will also have great remorse when they recognize who He really is, the very same Jesus of Nazareth, the carpenter's son, who was rejected, reviled, spat upon, beaten and finally crucified at the instigation of their high priests 2,000 years before. Their fathers had missed Him, they cry. They had missed the coming of their Messiah! They had not recognized Him when He had come!

What does He look like now? In Revelation 1:14-16 John gives us His description: "His head and his hairs were like wool, as white as snow; and his eyes were as a flame of fire; And his feet like unto fine brass, as if they burned in a furnace; and his voice as the sound of many waters. And he had in his right hand seven stars: and out of his mouth went a sharp two-edged sword: and his countenance was as the sun shineth in his strength."

Destruction of the Antichrist's Army

This is what the armies of the antichrist see astride the white horse. They gaze upon Him in fear and terror. The very earth under their feet shakes with the fury of the Lord. Ezekiel 38:21-22 tells us what happens next: "And I will call for a sword against him throughout all my mountains, saith the Lord God: every man's sword shall be against his brother. And I will plead against him with pestilence and with blood; and I will rain upon him, and upon his bands, and upon the many people that are with him, an overflowing rain, and great hailstones, fire, and brimstone."

Ezekiel 39:2 tells us how many of the army of the antichrist will survive the fury of the Lord, "And I will turn thee back, and leave but the sixth part of thee ...."

In Zechariah 14:12-13 we are given more details of what will happen on that day, "And this shall be the plague wherewith the Lord will smite all the people that have fought against Jerusalem; Their flesh shall consume away while they stand upon their feet, and their eyes shall consume away in their holes, and their tongues shall consume away in their mouth. And it shall come to pass in that day, that a great tumult from the Lord shall be among them; and they shall lay hold every one on the hand of his neighbor, and his hand shall rise up against the hand of his neighbor."

From these accounts of the Battle of Armageddon several things are very clear. First, Christ does not need *any* earthly soldiers to defeat the armies of the antichrist. There will not be any earthly army with Him when He defeats them. Out of His mouth comes a sharp, two-edged sword, which is the Word of God, and this alone is sufficient to destroy the enemy.

Second, when the Lord's feet touch the Mount of Olives there will be a great earthquake, accompanied by hail, fire and brimstone. The very same power with which the Lord destroyed Sodom and Gomorrah will be used against the army of the antichrist. Their flesh will be consumed as they stand, their eyes seared out of their sockets, and their tongues burned away in their mouths.

Third, they will be so seized with terror and panic that they will set on one another with their weapons and will kill each other. Only one-sixth of this army will escape and flee from the all-consuming truth of the Word of God.

But what of the antichrist and the false prophet? What will happen to them?

The Antichrist and the False Prophet

Revelation 19:20 tells us of the fate of these two beasts of Satan: "And the beast was taken, and with him the false prophet that wrought miracles before him, with which he deceived them that had received the mark of the beast, and them that worshipped his image. These both were cast into a lake of fire burning with brimstone."

The lake of fire into which these two are cast is the fate of all of the godless. This lake is much worse than hell, as we shall see later. The fire of this lake does not consume the flesh nor kill the one cast into it. This fire torments the one consigned to it forever, night and day, without respite. This is the fate of the antichrist and the false prophet. And others will join them there.

The Fate of Satan

Revelation 20:1-3: "And I saw an angel come down from heaven, having the key of the bottomless pit and a great chain in his hand. And he laid hold on the dragon, that old serpent, which is the Devil, and Satan, and bound him a thousand years, And cast him into the bottomless pit, and shut him up, and set a seal upon him, that he should deceive the nations no more, till the thousand years should be fulfilled: and after that he must be loosed a little season."

For a thousand years men and women will not be tempted by Satan. The earth will be ruled by the King of kings and Lord of lords and the dragon will not be able to interfere. This earth will again become a paradise.

The First Resurrection — The Seventh Trumpet Sounds

But who will populate this new earth during the millennium reign of Christ? This is where the 'rapture' passage of First Thessalonians rightly belongs, for it is now that the First Resurrection occurs, the resurrection of the righteous.

"For the Lord himself shall descend from heaven with a shout, with the voice of the archangel, and with the trump of God: and the dead in Christ shall rise first: Then we which are alive and remain shall be caught up together with them in the clouds, to meet the Lord in the air: and so shall we ever be with the Lord" (1 Thess. 4:16-17).

Judgment of Christians

We are given more details of those who are a part of this resurrection in Revelation 20:4, "And I saw thrones and they sat upon them, and judgment was given unto them: and I saw the souls of them that were beheaded for the witness of Jesus, and for the word of God, and which had not worshipped the beast, neither his image, neither had received his mark upon their foreheads, or in their hands; and they lived and reigned with Christ a thousand years."

If Christians are not to go through the Great Tribulation, how do you explain this passage of the Scriptures? These people who sit upon the judgment thrones *have gone through it.* Some were killed by the antichrist for their testimony of Jesus Christ. None had accepted the mark of the beast. If they had not gone through the Great Tribulation, they would not have had an opportunity either to be killed for their testimony or to refuse the mark of the beast.

In this resurrection, all will be judged. Many do not realize that *all* Christians will have to stand one day before the judgment seat of Christ and give an account for their lives. This will be in the same manner that the servants of the rich man had to account for the talents they had been entrusted with. Paul tells us of this judgment in his second letter to the Corinthian church: "For we must all appear before the judgment seat of Christ; that every one may receive the things done in his body, according to that he hath done, whether it be good or bad" (2 Cor. 5:10).

In the gospel of Luke, Jesus spoke of the faithful and unfaithful servants. He warns us of what to expect when we stand before Him in judgment. In Luke 12:48 we read: "...For unto whomsoever much is given, of him shall be much required...."

This is the judgment of Christians and we are told of it in Revelation 20:6: "Blessed and holy is he that hath part in the first resurrection: on such the second death hath no power, but they shall be priests of God and of Christ, and shall reign with him a thousand years."

This judgment by Christ is to determine the rewards which each Christian will receive. Some will receive crowns, and some, perhaps, will receive no reward at all. Paul told the Corinthians of this: "For other foundation can no man lay than is laid, which is Jesus Christ. Now if any man build upon this foundation gold, silver, precious stones, wood, hay, stubble; Every man's work shall be made manifest: for the day shall declare it, because it shall be revealed by fire; and the fire shall try every man's work of what sort it is. If any man's work abide which he hath built thereupon, he shall receive a reward. If any man's work shall be burned, he shall suffer loss: but he himself shall be saved; yet so as by fire" (1 Cor. 3:11-15).

Christ will judge our lives and our works. Our works will not save us; salvation comes solely by the grace of God and our belief in Jesus Christ, but according to our works rewards shall be given at this judgment by Christ.

The Millennial Earth

For most of my life I was taught that Christians would spend their eternity in heaven. I have heard sermons describing a beautiful place far up among fluffy, white clouds with a magnificent gate of pearl and streets of solid gold, palacial mansions and white-robed angels with folded wings. I even pictured Saint Peter standing at the entrance with a thick book, checking the names of those who desired entry into this heavenly splendor.

But this is *not* what the Bible tells us. Our eternity will be spent not up among the clouds, but right here on earth, an earth which has been purged by blood and fire and made clean and pure again by the return of Jesus Christ.

With Christ's Second Coming and the defeat of the antichrist and the chaining of Satan, the 1,000 years of the Millennium begins. We are told that Christians who have come through the Great Tribulation without losing their faith or succumbing to the lies of Satan, the antichrist or the false prophet, will rule with Him during this period. Many questions come immediately to mind.

After the horrible destruction of the Great Tribulation and the pouring out of God's wrath, what will the earth be like?

What will we be like? Will we have different bodies?

Who will make up the population of the earth during this time?

We are not given much specific information about these things in the Bible, but from what we have been given we can draw some conclusions. In any event, Jesus Christ will be here with us, so we do not have to be concerned about anything. He will be in complete control.

It is evident from the Revelation description of the plagues which will strike the earth during the Great Tribulation that the earth will be left in a terrible condition. The ravages of nuclear war, earthquakes, poisoned oceans and other bodies of water, destruction of most of the forests and grasslands will certainly leave the earth a most inhospitable place. But the very One who created this planet will be here with us, and it is in His power to change or renew the world in any manner He sees fit. We should have absolutely no concern about this.

First Corinthians 15:51-53 tells about the resurrection body: "Behold, I shew you a mystery; We shall not all sleep, but we shall all be changed. In a moment, in the twinkling of an eye, at the last trump: for the trumpet shall sound, and the dead shall be raised incorruptible, and we shall be changed. For this corruptible must put on incorruption, and this mortal must put on immortality."

Christians will have new resurrection bodies. But what of the others who are left on earth, what of those non-Christians left alive after the Battle of Armageddon? Certainly many of the inhabitants of the nations of the world will still be in the world alive; perhaps a billion people will be left. What is their fate during the Millennium?

The Bible does not tell us exactly what will happen to these people, but we may surmise that they will not have new bodies such as Christians will have. As we said before, the Millennium will be a time when the spiritual and physical planes of existence will merge. Both will live simultaneously on earth. These people will probably be subject to the limitations of the flesh. They will probably still bear children.

We are not told whether these people will suffer from disease and illness or whether they will die during the Millennium. Without Satan loose in the world, they will not be tempted to sin. But these people have a definite part in God's plan and we will examine what that is.

Satan Loosed for a Little Season

"And when the thousand years are expired, Satan shall be loosed out of his prison, And shall go out to deceive the nations which are in the four quarters of the earth, Gog and Magog, to gather them together to battle: the number of whom is as the sand of the sea. And they went up on the breadth of the earth, and compassed the camp of the saints about, and the beloved city: and fire came down from God out of heaven, and devoured them" (Rev. 20:7-9).

The mortals are allowed to remain on earth to give Satan another opportunity to work his lies and deceptions. Certainly the Christians in new resurrection bodies will not be tempted by Satan's lies, so that leaves the people from all the nations of the world after the Battle of Armageddon. Those who come up against the saints of God are destroyed by fire sent by God out of heaven.

Now Satan can be dealt with once and for all time: "And the devil that deceived them was cast into the lake of fire and brimstone, where the beast and the false prophet are, and shall be tormented day and night for ever and ever" (Rev. 20:10).

No more Satan. No more temptations. No more sin in the world.

The earth is now what God planned for it to be in the very beginning, a paradise for His people.

The Great White-Throne Judgment

Christians will be judged by Christ after the First Resurrection, the resurrection of the righteous. Now comes the Second Resurrection and the Great White-Throne Judgment. This is where the ungodly will receive their fate for all eternity.

"And I saw a great white throne, and him that sat upon it, from whose face the earth and the heaven fled away; and there was found no place for them. And I saw the dead, small and great, stand before God; and the books were opened: and another book was opened, which is the book of life: and the dead were judged out of those things which were written in the books, according to their works. And the sea gave up the dead which were in it; and death and hell delivered up the dead which were in them: and they were judged every man according to their works" (Rev. 20:11-13).

It is implied that everyone who stands before the Great White Throne of God during this judgment will be found guilty. These will suffer the Second Death, a final and ultimate sentencing for all of eternity.

"And death and hell were cast into the lake of fire. This is the second death. And whosoever was not found written in the book of life was cast into the lake of fire" (Rev. 20:14-15).

I have heard people question the mercy and goodness of God, asking why, if God is all-good and all-merciful, He would condemn people to spend an eternity in torment. But these people do not realize that it is not God condemning them to such an unspeakably horrible fate. Every person whose final destination is the lake of fire *has condemned himself to that fate.*

We are free and independent moral agents. We have the free choice between following God or following Satan. We ourselves choose to live or to die. We make the choice between good and evil. When we choose not to follow and obey God, we automatically choose Satan. There are no other options. It is not God who sentences us to everlasting torment, *we sentence ourselves!*

The End of Time

When the final trumpet sounds there will be no more time. What is then will be forever. Eternity will have begun. We have seen the final and eternal fate of the ungodly. Now we see where the Christians will spend eternity.

"And I saw a new heaven and a new earth: for the first heaven and the first earth were passed away; and there was no more sea. And I John saw the holy city, new Jerusalem, coming down from God out of heaven, prepared as a bride adorned for her husband. And I heard a great voice out of heaven saying, Behold, the tabernacle of God is with men, and he will dwell with them, and they shall be his people, and God himself shall be with them, and be their God" (Rev. 21:1-3).

The Beginning of Eternity

This will be the eternal home of Christians. There will be no more tears, no more unhappiness, no more tribulation. Imperfect bodies will be made perfect, the blind will see, the lame will walk, the deaf will hear. Revelation 21:4 tells us: "And God shall wipe away all tears from their eyes; and there shall be no more death, neither sorrow, nor crying, neither shall there be any more pain: for the former things are passed away."

Peter was also given a glimpse of this and he wrote: "But the day of the Lord will come as a thief in the night; in the which the heavens shall pass away with a great noise, and the elements shall melt with fervent heat, the earth also and the works that are therein shall be burnt up" (2 Pet. 3:10).

He goes on to caution us, "Seeing then that all these things shall be dissolved, what manner of persons ought ye to be in all holy conversation and godliness, Looking for and hasting unto the coming of the day of God, wherein the heavens being on fire shall be dissolved, and the elements shall melt with fervent heat?" (2 Pet. 3:11, 12).

Peter then tells of what John saw with regard to a new home for Christians. "Nevertheless we, according to his promises, look for new heavens and a new earth, wherein dwelleth righteousness" (2 Pet. 3:13).

New Jerusalem — the Bride of Christ

Revelation 21:9-10 states: "And there came unto me one of the seven angels which had the seven vials full of the seven last plagues, and talked with me, saying, Come hither, I will show thee the bride, the Lamb's wife. And he carried me away in the spirit to a great and high mountain, and shewed me that great city, the holy Jerusalem, descending out of heaven from God..."

This city, new Jerusalem, needs no sun or moon to light it, for it is illuminated by the brilliant light of the Lamb. There will never be darkness there.

For those who have given their lives — and souls — to Jesus Christ, and have made Him not only their Savior but their Lord as well, and have lived their lives as He has directed them, their eternal home will be the new Jerusalem. Theirs will be the everlasting joy it will bring. But to those who have not given their hearts to Jesus Christ, their eternal home will be the lake of fire and an eternity of torment from which there is no reprieve.

Our lives are not games in which if we choose the wrong side we can merely walk away and perhaps play again. The stakes here are immeasurably high — the fate we choose for all of eternity. We are free to choose either God or Satan, good or evil. The result will be either eternal reward or eternal punishment.

God will not make this choice for us. We must make this decision ourselves.

Summary of End-Times Events

I believe the Scriptures give us the following series of events in the last days:

1. The antichrist will be revealed. He will suffer the 'deadly wound' and recover. The false prophet will make his appearance on the world scene.

2. The Great Tribulation will begin. The antichrist will make war with the saints and conquer the world.

3. A one-world government will be established with the antichrist as supreme leader. All nations, with the exception of Israel, will be under the antichrist. A one-world false religion will be established, probably with the false prophet as its high priest.

4. Millions of Christians will refuse the mark of the beast and either be executed or die of starvation.

5. God will pour out His wrath upon the earth.

6. The antichrist will attack Israel.

7. The Seventh Trumpet, the final trump, will sound.

8. Christ will return to earth at the head of His heavenly army. The First Resurrection will occur and living Christians will receive resurrection bodies. The army of the antichrist will be destroyed; the antichrist and the false prophet will be cast into the Lake of Fire. Satan will be bound.

9. The saints will reign with Christ for a thousand years, while others on earth who have survived will probably lead natural lives.

10. At the end of the Millenium, Satan will be loosed for a short time to tempt the nations to attack the Holy City and the saints. They will surround the 'camp of the saints.'

11. God will destroy them with fire from heaven, and Satan will be cast into the Lake of Fire.

12. The Second Resurrection will occur. The unjust and evil will be raised to stand before the Great White Throne Judgment. The Book of Life and other books will be opened and the unjust will be judged out of these books. It is indicated from the Scriptures that none of these will be found in the Lamb's Book of Life and will be cast into the Lake of Fire, along with death and hell.

After these events, Christians will enjoy an eternity full of happiness and joy. Those of the Second Resurrection will enter an eternity of perpetual torment in the Lake of Fire.

15

Is This Really True?

Destiny is not a matter of chance, it is a matter of choice; it is not a thing to be waited for, it is a thing to be achieved. (William Jennings Bryan)

It isn't that they can't see the solution. It is that they can't see the problem. (G.K. Chesterton)

You have read the Revelation prophecy concerning the end times and those prophecies concerning the clues which we have been given to identify the antichrist. You have also examined the evidence concerning the present leader of the Soviet Union, Mikhail S. Gorbachev, and have seen that he fits exactly these prophetic clues.

We have calculated the probability of his name giving the specific theomatic numbers 666, 46 and 111. Now we will calculate the mathematical probability of Gorbachev fitting *all* of the antichrist prophecy possible so far in his life, including the hidden clues which we have examined.

We will use the individual assigned probabilities which are given in Exhibit IV and determine the probability of one man, Mikhail S. Gorbachev, meeting them all.

The Total Probability

The total probability of Gorbachev meeting all of the individual probabilities and hidden clues is calculated to be: 1 in 1,797,880,320,000,000,000.

This is 1 in one quintillion, seven hundred and ninety-seven quadrillion, eight hundred and eighty trillion, three hundred and twenty billion.

To get an idea just how large this number is, let us compare it with the population of the earth today. There are about five billion people living on the earth at this time. The mathematical probability of one person fitting all of the antichrist prophecy and the hidden clues which we have examined that show that Mikhail S. Gobachev indeed does fit, is the same as saying that only *one* person on 359,576,064 earths of the same population as ours would statistically meet them all. If we were to assume, and correctly so, that the antichrist would have to be an adult male, which is about one-fourth of the population, then this number of earths would be four times as many statistically, or 1,438,304,256 with the same population as ours would be required.

The Odds That He Is

Probability is not the same as odds, although the probability of something is used in the calculation of the odds that it will or will not happen. If we use the letter P to represent the probability of an occurrence, and x for the odds, then the odds are obtained using the following equation:

$$x = 1 - P/P$$

The odds that Gorbachev is actually the antichrist have also been calculated. This number, like the probability, is enormous. The calculations indicating the odds that Gorbachev is the actual and true antichrist are: 710,609,175,188,282,100 to 1.

This means that if you want to bet that Gorbachev is not the true antichrist, you will be betting against odds of seven hundred and ten quadrillion, six hundred and nine trillion, one hundred and seventy-five billion, one hundred and eighty-eight million, two hundred and eighty-two thousand, one hundred.

But there may be disagreement on the basic probabilities I have assigned to the individual cases shown in Exhibit IV. The probabilities of the linguistic clues, such as transliterations of his name being functions of the numbers 666, 46, 111 and 888 are direct. But the numerical probabilities of my estimate of 2,000 other men of equal age, background, etc. within the structure of the Soviet Communist Party who could have been selected for the rapid advancement which he experienced and who could have emerged as the leader of the Soviet Union could well be disputed. Other areas of potential disagreement would be the assigned probabilities of Gorbachev being the eighth 'king' or leader, the ten other 'kingdoms' under his control, and the existence of exactly seven Warsaw Pact nations.

In order to eliminate this possible disagreement and to prevent it from clouding the major issues, I have *reduced* the figures for both probability and odds. But how much should I reduce them?

By half? By two-thirds?

By 90 percent?

No! I have reduced both probability and odds by 99.999 percent.

Now, calculating the probability as only 0.001 percent of our original figures, we get:

Probability = 17,978,803,200,000

Odds = 7,106,091,751,882

You can readily see that even with these drastically reduced probabilities and odds, the statistics indicate overwhelmingly that Mikhail S. Gorbachev is the actual man which John saw rising from the sea — the antichrist.

Again, in terms of earths of the same population as our own, there would be only one person on over 3,500 earths like our own who would meet all of the antichrist requirements.

But Gorbachev does!

EXHIBIT IV

FEATURE	PROB-ABILITY	ODDS
1. Mikhail S. Gorbachev in Russian equals 666 x 2 (+/-3)	95	94
2. Mikhail S. Gorbachev in Russian equals 46 x 29 (+/-1)	15	14
3. Mikhail Gorbachev in Russian equals 46 x 27 (+/-3)	6	5
4. Mikhail S. Gorbachev in Greek equals 888 x 2 (+/-1)	296	295
5. Gorbachev in Greek equals exactly 888	888	887
6. Rise from obscurity over men of equal qualifications	2000	1999
7. Soviet population exactly 276 million (Satan's number)	50	49
8. Rules ten other kingdoms	10	9
9. Exactly ten kings (Politburo members when elected)	10	9
10. Exactly seven Warsaw Pact nations	10	9
11. Being the eighth 'king' or leader of the USSR	8	7

Calculations

Probability: (95) (15) (6) (296) (888) (2000) (50) (10) (10) (10) (8)
1 person in 1,797,880,320,000,000,000

Odds: (94) (14) (5) (295) (887) (1999) (49) (9) (9) (9) (7)
1 chance in 710,609,175,188,282,100 of a person meeting the above mathematical probabilities and odds and *not* being the antichrist.

Natural Disbelief

If you agree with the evidence presented here, even if you strongly feel that the end times are indeed upon us, but in the back of your mind there still lingers a disbelief of the catastrophic events which will be a part of them — I can understand.

No one wants to believe that within the next ten years or so everything around them will be gone. We are so entrenched in our lives and the way things have been for so long that we have a natural and understandable tendency to believe they will go on like this forever.

Jesus knew this when He said in Luke 17:26-29: "And as it was in the days of Noe, so shall it be in the days of the Son of man. They did eat, they drank, they married wives, they were given in marriage, until the day that Noe entered into the ark, and the flood came, and destroyed them all. Likewise also as it was in the days of Lot; they did eat, they drank, they bought, they sold, they planted, they builded; But the same day that Lot went out of Sodom it rained fire and brimstone from heaven, and destroyed them all."

No one today wants even to contemplate what is coming. We *want* to believe in a future where our children will grow up, marry, have our grandchildren. We look ahead perhaps to retirement, some to fulfillment of our plans for a career. None of us wants to look squarely at the Revelation prophecy and admit that there will be no time to accomplish these things.

Even Christians who say that they are looking forward to the return of Jesus Christ do not want to think of what they and their loved ones must go through before He can come again.

Belief or Faith?

Many people today in our churches believe *in* God, but they do not *believe God.* They do not believe He will do as He has said He will. The Revelation prophecy which we have examined is just as much the prophetic word of God, given through John the apostle, as any prophecy of the Old Testament which has already been fulfilled. And just as what Jeremiah, Isaiah, Daniel, Ezekiel and other men of God prophesied has happened — so will the antichrist conquer the world.

Still, we have a natural, mental resistance to believing that this is actually going to happen *to us.* It was well and good for God's prophecy to bring catastrophe to *other* people in *another* time — but *not to us!*

One Sunday morning a preacher asked his congregation, "How many of you want to go to heaven?" Everyone's hand shot up. Then he asked another question. "How many of you want to go *right now?*" Not one hand was raised.

Even if our life is hard, even if we have not achieved in life what we dreamed of achieving, we are still reluctant to let go of it. Some people each year choose to end their lives, but the vast majority of us cling to life tenaciously, unwilling to give up even the most meager and painful existence.

Why believe this world is now coming to a close? Hasn't history been full of such predictions which have never happened? Haven't people made fools of themselves in the past by believing this sort of thing?

Yes, they have. Even the Thessalonians quit their jobs and sat around on a hill waiting for the immediate return of Jesus Christ. They had misinterpreted Paul's letter to them and he had to hurriedly correct them. Then why believe this now?

The reason we should believe that this will happen now, within the next few years, is that God's Word has given us the signs to look for and they are all present at this time. Everything is in place. All that had to happen first has happened. Those who falsely predicted the end of the world in times past did not pay attention to the Word of God. They relied on some sort of 'psychic revelation' instead of the Word of the very One who created all this in the beginning and controls it *right now as He has all along.*

To give you a concrete example of how much God is in control at this very moment, I want to share something with you which was reported by *The New York Times* recently concerning the Soviet Nuclear disaster at Chernobyl.

The Chernobyl Disaster — a Message From God

The Chernobyl nuclear power station is near the city of Kiev in the Soviet Ukraine. We all know about the accident there which released radiation that spread radioactive fallout over a wide path in northern Europe. The danger still exists of contamination of the water supply of Kiev by the radioisotopes released when the core of the reactor burned. The Russians are trying to intercept ground water before it passes through the contaminated area around the plant and then goes on to the lake and the Dnieper River.

Now let us go back to God's Word in Revelation 8:10-11 where the third angel sounds a trumpet and a star named Wormwood falls into the rivers and fountains of waters, which are underground streams. This star, Wormwood, so poisoned these fresh waters that many died from drinking them.

In the Ukraine there grows an herb which is commonly called *wormwood*. The name for this herb in the Ukrainian language is CHERNOBYL.

God is telling us, through this Soviet nuclear disaster, exactly what the star named Wormwood in Revelation really is — nuclear contamination from a nuclear war which will poison the third part of the earth's drinking water.

But this tells us something else. It shows this unbelieving generation that He has been in control all along and is still in complete control of the events of this world.

First, God was in control of the Ukrainian language so that this common bitter herb was named Chernobyl.

Secondly, the town in the Ukraine where the power station would be built years later had to be named Chernobyl.

Third, He had to influence the Soviets to choose to construct this four-unit nuclear power station at the town called Chernobyl.

And last, this nuclear accident had to occur, threatening the water supply of Kiev and the Dnieper River.

Can't you see God's hand in all of this, absolutely in control during all these years of events, even down to the naming of the common herb?

If He is in control of *these* things, then He is in control of *all* things.

Can Anything Be Done to Prevent This From Happening?

No! God has determined that these catastrophic events will take place in the last few years of this world as we now know it, and God's will *will* be done. Nothing that man — or Satan — can do will prevent God's plan from taking place.

Why Is This Happening Now?

In our examination of the biblical prophecy concerning the end times we read in God's Word about those events, such as the reestablishment of Israel, which had to come before the antichrist would make his appearance on the world scene. We have seen that biblical prophecy made 2,500 years ago gave the names of the very nations which have lined up against this nation of God's chosen people in preparation for the last and final battle of Armageddon. We have witnessed the Soviet Union building the military might by which the antichrist will conquer the world, but we are now presented with another unusual aspect of God's timing for the end of the world.

Do you remember that we found the number six to represent the world in God's numerical system? This number has special significance for us today.

The first man the Bible speaks of is Adam.

God made His covenant with another man, Abraham.

From Adam to Abraham was 2,000 years.

From Abraham to the birth of God's Son was 2,000 years.

Jesus was born in 5 BC.

From Jesus' birth to our year 1995 will be exactly another 2000 years.

This gives us a total of 6,000 years for the lifespan of the biblical earth. This world has used up all of the time which God has allotted to it. The next thousand years will be the Millennium, when this earth will be ruled by Christ. The number seven denotes perfection, and at the end of 7,000 years God will have perfected a multitude of men and women with which to populate the New Jerusalem for all eternity.

But There Is Something That You Can Do!

It is entirely within your power to choose where you will spend your eternity. Death does *not* involve going into a state of perpetual unconsciousness. God's Word tells us that we will *know* exactly where we are. We will be able to experience the emotions of joy and happiness — and we will also be capable of feeling pain and suffering. Where we spend our eternity will determine whether we find complete happiness forever — or eternal torment.

That choice *must* be made now. We either decide right now to give our lives to Jesus Christ or to Satan. There is no other option, for to reject Christ is to choose Satan, and to consign our souls to the lake of fire with him.

By an act of our free wills, we must accept the sacrifice Jesus made on the cross for us and make Him Lord of our lives. We must get to know Him *personally* in this life, or He will not acknowledge us when we stand before Him in judgment. No church can save you. Baptism will not save you. Only by *sincerely* giving our lives to His control can we assure ourselves of an eternity with Him instead of being in the lake of fire with Satan, the antichrist, the false prophet and the ungodly.

But we must really mean it. Unfortunately, many who sit in church every Sunday are under the delusion that they have been saved from the fire. But unless they have given their hearts and their lives *sincerely* to Jesus Christ and live for Him, they are mistaken.

In Matthew 7:21-23, Jesus told of the fate of many like this: "Not everyone who saith unto me, Lord, Lord, shall enter into the kingdom of heaven; but he that doeth the will of my Father which is in heaven. Many will say to me in that day, Lord, Lord, have we not prophesied in thy name? and in thy name have cast out devils? and in thy name done many wonderful works? And then I will profess unto them, I never knew you: depart from me, ye that work iniquity."

To enter into His kingdom, we must know Jesus Christ on a personal basis in this life, or He will *not know us then*. There won't be a second chance. What you do now will determine where you will be for all eternity.

Get to know Him now! It is a frightening thing to contemplate, but for each of us our eternity is but a single heartbeat away.

Get ready now. Get to know Jesus Christ.

The Great Tribulation is coming quickly upon us.

Christians will have to go through it.

There will not be a pre-tribulation rapture, no matter what you have been taught.

Get yourself and your loved ones spiritually ready to face it.

Precious little time remains.

In conclusion, I want to go back to the Ukraine again, to the city of Kiev. Just a few months prior to the Chernobyl nuclear disaster, Christians in Kiev saw a bright light in the northern sky coming from the direction of the nuclear power station. As they watched, this light took on the shape of a fish —the ancient Christian symbol. Then a brilliantly colored rainbow formed around the fish.

Then the most astonishing thing of all happened. A sentence appeared in the sky in Russian, saying, "I AM COMING SOON."

And as John said as he concluded his book, "Amen. Even so, come, Lord Jesus" (Rev. 22:20).

Appendix

The Fall of America — a Possible Scenario

The following scenario is written in "You Are There" fashion in order to give us a feeling of what life will be like during The Great Tribulation. This material is not meant to be a literal prophecy, but it does develop several possibilities worthy of our consideration. It is quite likely that some of these events *will* take place, and it is certain that similar situations will develop, but we do not mean to suggest that this scenario portrays the actual chain of events leading to the return of our Lord.

There is a downturn in the American economy. Despite efforts by the administration, this crisis worsens month by month. Major changes in weather patterns result in widespread crop losses in the South and Midwest. The number of farmers forced into bankruptcy increases by fourfold. Many small banks, their reserves inadequate to handle these loan forfeitures, go down with the farmers. The Federal Deposit Insurance Corporation reserves are totally incapable of sustaining these bank failures. Congress is forced to enact legislation to repay depositors of these banks, but there is panic. Many banks experience a run of withdrawals by depositors.

Plant closings and layoffs result in increasing unemployment. A dozen major U.S. corporations are on the verge of bankruptcy. They blame foreign imports and Congress enacts stringent protectionist legislation. Foreign markets reciprocate with their own trade restrictions.

Third World countries, especially the smaller oil producers, have been hit hard by depressed oil prices and begin to default on international loans, requesting rescheduling and additional loans with which to pay interest on current loans. The world financial community, already in serious trouble, refuses. Mexico and Brazil declare bankruptcy and disavow their U.S. obligations. The two largest American banks flounder, their reserves insufficient to cover these defaults. The federal government is unable to help either the major banks or major corporations to stay afloat.

The Nicaraguan Contras ceased to exist after Congress cut off all aid to them. Nicaraguan troops cross the border into Honduras and El Salvador, claiming that they are pursuing rebel forces. In both countries, communist guerilla forces attempt a takeover. Congress debates sending in U.S. Marines. While the debate goes on, both Honduras and El Salvador are lost to the communists.

There is a communist-led insurrection in the Philippines. The communist rebels threaten the American naval base at Subic Bay. The Aquino government falls.

The decline in the U.S. economy is felt in Europe and a deepening recession is also felt there. Higher oil prices instituted by OPEC nations of the Middle East further aggravate the situation. In the U.S. both the balance of payments and budget deficit continue to climb. Congress blames the administration for the deteriorating situation. A liberal president is elected who promises the return of a healthy American economy.

Sweeping agreements have been made between the United States and the Soviet Union on nuclear arms reduction. All short- and medium- range nuclear weapons have been eliminated and a reduction of 50 percent in long-range strategic warheads has been agreed upon by both powers. This is hailed by the world press as greatly reducing tension and the threat of nuclear war. The United States asks the other NATO allies to bear an increased cost of European defense. They refuse.

In the United States the AIDS epidemic rages unchecked. It is estimated that eight million Americans have been exposed to the AIDS virus. Deaths have reached 200,000 and are climbing. The public panics, demanding more money for research to find a cure. But with the declining economy and soaring deficits, there is very little money available for medical research.

The Mexican government falls to a leftist coup. Immediately a million Mexicans storm across the border into the United States, with more following each month. Humanitarian groups call for government money to feed and house these 'political refugees.' Congress can find no funds to appropriate.

As the communist forces in Central America threaten other nations in the area, Congress belatedly authorizes U.S. forces to intervene. After strong initial public support, Americans begin to have second thoughts when the landing of Marine and Army units is met with unexpectedly fierce resistance, resulting in heavy casualties.

Terrorists bomb several American embassies, killing one U.S. ambassador. The demand for ceasing this terrorist activity is that the U.S. stop aid to Israel. An American jet is blown up over the Atlantic, killing all 435 on board. The U.S. experiences the most severe winter in 100 years; heating bills for Americans soar with the ever-increasing price of oil. Some Congressmen propose U.S. military intervention in the Middle East to stabilize oil prices.

Month by month U.S. casualties grow in Central America. It is confirmed that Cuban troops are involved. The Secretary of Defense wants to invade Cuba, but the Soviets state that any action against Cuba would be considered an act of war against the Soviet Union. The U.S. backs down.

Summer brings another poor agricultural season. Swarms of grasshoppers plague crops in the upper Midwest while insufficient rainfall in the South gives low crop yields. Foreclosures hit a record high. Public and private funds for relief run out. Congress considers food rationing. A terrorist bomb explodes in downtown Washington, killing fifty people. Fall brings severe cold to most of the nation. In November snow falls in Alabama and Mississippi. Retail stores report slow sales at Christmas.

Spring brings torrential rains to the Northwest. Thousands are left homeless as a result of floods. U.S. troops are pushed back in a spring offensive by Nicaraguan and Cuban troops. Crowds jam Washington streets, demanding a U.S. pullout. More large U.S. corporations fail, forcing another 200,000 workers onto the unemployment rolls.

The AIDS epidemic continues. It is estimated that by now over sixteen million Americans have been exposed to the disease. Deaths this year are expected to exceed 500,000. No vaccine or cure has been found.

Mexicans continue to pour illegally over the border. Estimates now show that at least four million Mexicans have sought refuge here. Citizen committees in Southwest arm themselves to prevent Mexicans from entering their towns. The Red Cross and other agencies have been overwhelmed. Congress does not increase funds, claiming that U.S. citizens should have the first right to assistance.

Crime has risen alarmingly, with robbery and larceny up fourfold. The number of Americans committing suicide has tripled over the last year. Publicly funded abortions are now at three million per year.

Geologists warn that there are signs that the huge underground aquifers are being depleted. Many wells are now dry and the flow of the Colorado River has been reduced by half.

Winter brought a sever influenza epidemic to North America, affecting over half the population to some degree. Hospitals are overcrowded. Deaths have topped 250,000 with the very young and the very old being its main victims. Scientists say this strain of the virus is potentially more dangerous than that of the influenza epidemic of 1918-19, which killed thirty million people worldwide.

Spring was marked by demonstrations demanding U.S. withdrawal of troops from Central America, not only in this country but in Europe as well. The American casualties have now topped 25,000 dead and 250,000 wounded. In May the President announced that a cease fire had been agreed upon and that American withdrawal would begin immediately.

By summer it became clear that a Marxist regime had been set up in Mexico, with Soviet and Cuban aid being received. Stories of civil rights violations there prompt Congress to demand that the United Nations investigate. Soviet-bloc countries defeat this. Now it is estimated that at least ten million illegal Mexican aliens are in this country. Continual violence occurs between these people and the armed citizens of the Southwestern states. In one incident, over 100 Mexicans were killed as they tried to enter a Texas town, The government seems not to be capable of handling this situation.

An earthquake of 6.4 on the Richter scale rocks Southern California, causing an estimated $500 million in damage and killing sixty-four people. Seismologists warn that this may be the precursor of an even-larger quake. Mount St. Helens erupts again, spewing ash over a wide area of the Northwest. Near Palmdale, California, the earth has risen fourteen feet in the last three years over an area of one hundred square miles. Seismologists are greatly concerned.

OPEC announces another price increase in crude oil to fifty-five dollars per barrel. Americans are cutting trees in parks and state forest reserves for firewood. State police do nothing to prevent this. National Guard troops are called in to prevent Mexican immigrants from entering downtown Dallas and looting stores. Rioting breaks out in several northern cities. Alaska records an increasing number of small earth tremors, but scientists are concerned because they seem to be increasing in intensity. Forest rangers report deer and other animals acting in an unusual manner, as are household pets.

By winter the climate was slightly milder than the previous winter, but the influenza returned. In January the total deaths from influenza had reached 950,000 in the United States and fifteen million worldwide, despite the use of vaccines. AIDS continues to ravage this country, with an estimated thirty-two million Americans now infected with the virus. It is predicted that two million will die from this disease in the U.S. during the coming year.

All American nuclear weapons have been removed from Europe and the number of U.S. servicemen attached to NATO is now only twenty-five thousand. The national debt has risen to almost four trillion dollars with a huge deficit expected again this year. Taxes are again raised and Congress has passed legislation reducing Social Security benefits by one-third. This was necessary, the President states, in order for the U.S. government to remain solvent. There is talk in financial circles about the government defaulting on savings bonds and long-term securities. The administration denies this.

An earthquake of unimaginable magnitude strikes the West Coast of the United States. All communications are immediately lost from California, Oregon, Washington and Alaska. The jolt is felt in Chicago, St. Louis and as far as Cleveland and Dallas. Seismic stations around the world record this quake and scientists are shocked as their equipment measures a quake at least a thousand times stronger than any previous quake in history.

The first word on the extent of the disaster came from the GOES-6 weather satellite over the Pacific Ocean, indicating an enormous cloud of dust, smoke and debris covering the entire West Coast from Baja, California, to Alaska and extending far inland.

Aftershocks were recorded as high as 8.8 on the Richter scale by seismic stations. The Pacific Tsunami Warning Center issued immediate warnings for all residents of the Hawaiian Islands to seek shelter on high ground because of the danger of tidal waves. Network television recorded the voices of the crews of aircraft flying over Los Angeles and San Francisco. "It's gone," one pilot murmured with a wavering voice. "Nothing's left! Just rubble and ruin!"

The West Coast of the United States no longer exists. The waters of the Pacific Ocean now cover much of the land as far inland as the Sierra Nevadas and Cascade ranges. The destruction was total, complete, absolute — with few survivors. The American public in the rest of the country sat in paralyzed shock before television screens as the worst natural disaster in recorded history was revealed, bit by bit.

The shock wave raced westward through the Pacific Ocean at a speed approaching 600 miles per hour. Surprisingly, ships at sea were unaware of the shock waves as they passed beneath them, their peaks and troughs less than a foot higher or lower than ordinary waves. In less than four hours they had reached Hawaii. As the force struck shallow water, a wall of water over five hundred feet high lunged upward, striking all that was before it with the power of an enormous sledgehammer. Concrete buildings were smashed to bits as the huge wave surged inland.

A television crew set up their cameras on a hill overlooking Honolulu, broadcasting by satellite. The wave first obliterated the eastern side of the island, then snaked around Makapuu Head and swallowed Honolulu. At Pearl Harbor, ships of the U.S. Navy had put to sea as soon after the alert as possible. But one destroyer had not yet cleared the harbor and American television viewers saw this ship picked up like a toy boat and thrown two miles inland by the giant wall of water.

But this first wave was only the beginning. The second struck minutes later and was even more powerful than the first. Buildings weakened by the initial crash of water were splintered by the second, even higher and mightier wall of water. In the less than three hours of warning to get to high ground, only a fraction of the residents of the islands had succeeded in reaching safety. Cars and trucks had jammed the narrow roads leading upward into the hills. American viewers watched in horror as the third wave, some forty-eight minutes later and over a thousand feet high, swept across Oahu, wiping it clean of all evidence of human habitation. The other islands of the Hawaiian chain suffered the identical fate. Only a handful of people had made it to ground high enough to escape the utter carnage which swept the lush, green vegetation, the gleaming concrete towers, the rows of small homes, and the fertile volcanic soil away into the foaming billows of the Pacific.

Altogether, eight huge tidal waves and dozens of smaller ones ravaged the islands. Nor was Hawaii alone in this devastation. The towns on the Aleutians were swept clean by towering waves generated by the monster earthquake.

The American people sat in dazed silence as they witnessed the obliteration of over thirty million of their fellow citizens in but a few short hours. California was gone, Washington and Oregon had all but disappeared. The Hawaiian Islands had been devastated and over 80 percent of the state's population was dead — vanished into the boiling cauldron of the violent sea. The United States had been dealt a death blow by this unprecedented natural disaster. It would never recover. The United States was finished as a world power.

Only the nuclear armed missiles in their silos remained.

Inland, for hundreds of miles from the quake area, lay cities and towns which had been devastated. Relief agencies responded as best they could but the damage and destruction was so widespread that they were spread very thin. Canada, which had also suffered from the quake with the loss of life in Vancouver and smaller coastal cities, was in no position to assist the United States. With the horrendous damage of the quake, most of the country's aerospace, electronic and aircraft industry had been swallowed up, along with all military, naval and Air Force bases on the West Coast.

In March an incident in Poland so inflamed the Polish people that they revolted enmasse against their communist regime. The Polish Army joined the rebellion and Polish troops occupied Warsaw, deposing the communist leaders and proclaiming a democratic state. The Soviets were caught completely off-guard by this swift action and did not immediately respond. It was three weeks before Soviet tanks rumbled into Poland. They were repulsed with heavy casualties by Polish forces. The new Polish government called out to the Free World for assistance, and the world watched and waited, but could offer nothing but encouragement.

The two Soviet tank divisions stationed in Poland had been surprised by the Poles and had been captured, including many tanks, artillery pieces, ammunition and small arms. The Polish army consisted of one airborne division, four tank divisions and eight motorized infantry divisions. These units formed a ring of steel around Warsaw, knowing that they were not capable of defending the entire country against the Soviet and Warsaw Pact forces. In the Kremlin, Gorbachev faced opposition when he would not call on Czech and East German troops to invade Poland. He did not trust them, he told the Politburo. Soviet troops were sufficient to crush the Polish rebellion.

The Soviet Twentieth Tank Army sent elements into Poland, racing toward Poznan. But Polish men and women had manned the tanks and weapons captured from the two Russian tank divisions and met the Soviet forces at the Warta River, stopping them cold. In the east, the Soviet troops attacked the Polish army near Warsaw and were again repulsed. Rumors reached Western ears that Czechoslovakian troops had revolted, and there were demonstrations in East Germany and Hungary which had to be put down forcibly by Soviet soldiers.

By the first of June it was apparent that Gorbachev's leadership was in deep trouble. The Poles still held out and additional Soviet divisions had not been able to penetrate the ring of steel which had been placed around Warsaw. Reports of civil unrest, even within the Soviet Union, reached the West. It was quite apparent that the Soviet Union was suffering great humiliation by the Poles, and their valiant effort and initial success was prompting other Warsaw Pact nations to review their positions. A tight news blackout covered the Kremlin, but leaks suggested that Gorbachev was about to lose his position as supreme leader. The world waited and wondered. Was the mighty Soviet Union breaking apart?

On the 23rd of June the radio stations in Warsaw went off the air. Satellite pictures of the area indicated that a gigantic explosion had taken place. Seismic instruments indicated that a nuclear detonation had gone off. Radiation monitors suddenly came to life. Then it was clear what had transpired — the Soviets had destroyed Warsaw with a nuclear weapon. The world was shocked. No one had suspected that the Russians would do such a thing.

Moscow issued a statement, "The Polish problem has been resolved."

That summer the United States reeled under the effects of the great West Coast disaster, severe food shortages, raging unemployment, the problem of illegal Mexican aliens, and a treasury near bankruptcy. Police were unable to control the rampant crime; hospitals were filled to overflowing with the dying — from AIDS and influenza, along with malnutrition and mental illness. Entire families were committing suicide together.

The American people were dazed, bewildered, in the depths of despair — seemingly unable to cope with what was happening to them. Garbage collection ceased in many cities as there was not enough money to pay the collectors. Stores were looted by angry mobs. Most people were afraid to venture out of doors during the day, and no one except criminals dared it after dark. Chaos ruled the streets and panic gripped the citizens. What had happened? Why had these unthinkable things suddenly occurred in America? What had gone wrong?

In most churches the ministers and priests could not reassure or comfort their congregations. Church attendance fell off drastically, with only the most devout venturing out of their homes to attend services. In Philadelphia one man suddenly arose from his pew and proclaimed himself to be Jesus Christ. He pulled a pistol from his jacket and shot the pastor and two deacons before being subdued.

The Final Blow

The final stroke was delivered which completed the fall of the United States from a world power to a completely helpless nation. The Soviet Union launched a first strike against American-based missiles, military and naval installations, and SAC airfields.

The Soviet attack was superbly orchestrated. With split-second timing, Soviet forces struck around the globe. Russian commando units, called *spetsnaz*, had landed in various points undetected during the last week. Several of these had come ashore in Sweden by submarine, trekked across to U.S. satellite-receiving centers in Norway on the Vetan Peninsula and at Vadsø and destroyed them, effectually blinding the United States by eliminating the real-time transmission of our KH-11, SDS, and other satellites which keep watch on Warsaw Pact and Soviet actions. Other units struck installations at various points in Europe, while saboteurs destroyed similar satellite-receiving stations at Pine Gap and Nurrungar in Australia.

Soviet satellites which had long been considered out of service suddenly sprang back to life, changing their orbits to home in on American ELINT, PHOTINT, TELINT and other satellites in orbit around the earth. These anti-satellite weapons closed rapidly and when they were close enough, they exploded — sending a destructive hail of steel balls into the American space platforms keeping watch on the world below. The United States was completely blinded.

One of the Soviet ferret satellites swooped down to an orbit which took it 250 miles above Chicago. The 100-megaton warhead it contained detonated. Instantly there was a power failure in the continental power grid, blacking out most of North America. In addition, the wires of motors, generators, automobiles, and electrical equipment were burned out over most of the United States and Canada by the electromagnetic pulse from the 100-megaton space blast of the Soviet hydrogen device.

Only a few moments later Soviet warheads screamed out of the sky and exploded on U.S. missile silos, SAC airfields, military installations and submarine bases, in the continental United States and the islands in the Pacific and Indian Oceans and elsewhere in the Free World. Soviet attack and killer submarines launched nuclear torpedoes and depth bombs to destroy the American nuclear submarine they had been tracking.

The nuclear attack on the United States had left most major population areas intact, which would suffer fallout radiation but escape direct nuclear destruction. This had been part of the Soviet plan — to have over two-hundred million Americans held as nuclear hostages for the second part of their war plan.

The Red Phone, the direct line of communication between the White House and the Kremlin, rang and was answered. At the same time, as a precautionary measure in case this connection had been damaged, the Soviet ambassador arrived at the White House with a sealed message for the President of the United States.

The President was immediately aroused from sleep. The Soviet message was simple and direct. It stated that any retaliation — by a single U.S. warhead — would result in the total and complete destruction of all American cities of over 50,000 population by remaining Soviet nuclear missiles. The President, awakened out of a sound sleep to hear this message, put his head in his hands and wept, knowing that Gorbachev would do exactly what he said. Any retaliation would bring total and absolute destruction on the over one-hundred and fifty million Americans still alive.

The Soviet ambassador's note gave detailed instructions. Any remaining U.S. nuclear submarines were to surface immediately, all SAC bombers in the air were to return to the one U.S. airbase which the

Soviets had intentionally not destroyed. The President issued these instructions directly to the underground command post deep within the safety of the Colorado Rockies. The shielded fibre-optic telephone lines directly to military command centers had survived the electro-magnetic waves which had paralyzed all other communications. There would be no U.S. retaliation. The United States had, for all practical purposes, surrendered.

While the American public was held hostage to the threat of nuclear annihilation, a large proportion of Soviet citizens were deep under the earth in well-stocked shelters capable of surviving nuclear war. Under Moscow and under the beltway around it, the Politburo, their families and the leaders of the Soviet government were safely hidden beneath huge reinforced concrete bunkers and command posts.

The residents of the huge apartment buildings constructed since 1955 were also safe, in the system of underground shelters beneath their buildings. Tunnels connected these shelters and gave access to large storage rooms stocked with sufficient food, water and supplies for a prolonged stay. Diesel generators, vented to the air above, would furnish electric power and run the charcoal-filtered air supply system. Similar underground bunkers had been provided for factories and residents of most major cities. Even if the United States decided to retaliate, the Soviet Union was prepared to survive the nuclear war.

The Future

This scenario is not expected to be an actual, event by event, picture of the fall of the United States as a global power and the elimination of the American nuclear deterrent. I am quite certain that it will be somewhat different in time as well as sequence of events. But *something very like it will occur.* The Revelation prophecy demands it. God has already put into motion the things which will bring about His plan for the final days of the earth as we now know it. And it will happen just as His plan dictates.

As we read the Bible we find that time after time God has told the world what is to happen. Many times He has given His people a chance to repent, to mend their ways, to return to Him. But when His patience was exhausted, when his call for repentance went unheeded, when man continued on following Satan's dictates instead of God's — what His prophets had foretold *did come about.*

We are in the final few years of time. This earth will make but a scant few more revolutions around our star before the events of the end times prophecy come about. We have already entered that period of time when cataclysmic events, unrivaled troubles, great sorrow, and horrendous suffering will befall this planet and its people.

These things must happen. *God has said they will!*

And all the universe is in His hands.

These *are* the last days of earth.

What Would Happen If American Repents?

During the last several decades I believe God has raised up prophets to call the United States to repentance. God's Word has not returned void; many, many *individuals* have indeed repented. But this nation as a whole has not. God has told us, "If my people, which are called by my name, shall humble themselves, and pray, and seek my face, and turn from their wicked ways; then will I hear from heaven, and will forgive their sin, and will heal their land" (2 Chron. 7:14).

God is not only omnipotent, having all power; but He is also omniscient, knowing all things, even those things of the future. Even as He offered to hear America's prayers if the country would humble itself and repent, He *knew in advance* that the nation as a whole would not repent. This nation, more blessed by God than any other in history, will suffer the consequences of turning away from God and serving mammon.

Then There Is No Hope At All?

Yes! There *is* hope! And more than just hope, there is certainty. For God has provided you and me and every other human being alive today with the certainty of escape from the wrath of God's judgment.

"He that believeth on the Son hath everlasting life: and he that believeth not the Son shall not see life; but the wrath of God abideth on him" (John 3:36).

We may have to face the wrath of Satan in these last days, but that is nothing compared to the wrath of God. Satan's wrath is temporary; God's wrath is everlasting. Place your trust, your future, in the hands of the One whose hands *hold* the future: Jesus Christ, the King of kings and Lord of lords, the Son of God.

Your Future

You have within your power the ability to decide your own future. You can also influence the future of your loved ones and friends. The events described in this book have already been set in motion. Nothing that you or I can do will stop them. But we can determine our own future.

If you have not already given yourself totally to Jesus Christ, heart, mind and soul: then lay aside everything that prevents you from doing this and *do it now*. This is absolutely the most important decision in your life. He is standing just outside the door of your heart.

Open that door and let Him in.

He brings with Him everlasting life.

References

INTRODUCTION

(1) *THE LIVING BIBLE*; copyright 1971 by Tyndale House Publishers, Wheaton, IL. Used by permission.

CHAPTER ONE

(1) *THEOMATICS*, copyright 1977 by Jerry Lucas and Del Washburn. Material used with permission of Stein and Day, Publishers.

(2) *THE INTERLINEAR GREEK-ENGLISH NEW TESTAMENT*; by Alfred Marshall; Published by Zondervan Publishing House; Grand Rapids, Michigan 1975

(3) *HUGO'S RUSSIAN GRAMMAR SIMPLIFIED*; published by David McKay Company; Philadelphia, PA.

CHAPTER TWO

(1) *YOU CAN TRUST THE COMMUNISTS - TO DO EXACTLY WHAT THEY SAY*; by Dr. Fred Schwarz; Published by Prentice-Hall; Englewood Cliffs, New Jersey, 1960

(2) *THE GULAG ARCHIPELAGO*; by Aleksandr Solzhenitsyn; Published by Harper and Row, Inc. New York, New York 1953.

CHAPTER FOUR

(1) *ANDROPOV*; by Zhores A. Medvedev; Published by W.W. Norton and Co. New York, New York 1983. See also *Gorbachev*, by the same author and publisher.

CHAPTER FIVE

(1) Mikhail Tspkin; reported in an article in *CHRISTIAN INQUIRER*; Volume 16, No. 1; February 1986.

(2) *OPEN DOORS NEWS BRIEF*; Brother Andrew; Article by Jan Otto entitled "Who Stands Behind the Smiling Face?; Volume 1, Issue 6; July 1986.

CHAPTER SEVEN

(1) Figures of earthquakes and storms taken from: *THE WORLD ALMANAC AND BOOK OF FACTS*, 1986 Edition; copyright (c) Newspaper Enterprise Association, Inc. 1985, New York, N.Y. 10166

(2) *WEEKLY WORLD NEWS*; 600 South East Coast Avenue, Latana, FL. 33462 Used by permission

CHAPTER EIGHT

(1) *A SCIENTIFIC APPROACH TO CHRISTIANITY*; by Robert W. Faid; Published by Bridge Publishing, Inc., S.Plainfield, N.J.

CHAPTER ELEVEN

(1) *DEEP BLACK*; by William E. Burrows; Published by Random House, N.Y.

CHAPTER TWELVE

(1) *PEACE, PROSPERITY AND THE COMING HOLOCAUST; THE NEW AGE MOVEMENT IN PROPHECY*; by David Hunt; Published by Harvest House Publishers; Eugene, Oregon 1983

CHAPTER THIRTEEN

(1) *THE HISTORY OF THE CHURCH*; by Eusebius; translated by C.A. Williamson; Published by Penguin Books, N.Y., N.Y.

(2) *THE ANTI-NICENE FATHERS*; Volume 1, page 656, U.S. Edition 1979, Published by Wm. B. Eerdmans Publishing Co., Grand Rapids, MI. Used by permission

(3) *THE INCREDIBLE COVER-UP*; by Dave MacPherson; Published by Omega Publications; Medford, Oregon. Used by permission.

(4) *CHRISTIANS WILL GO THROUGH THE TRIBULATION*; by Dr. Jim McKeever; Published by Omega Publication; Medford, Oregon. Used by permission

CHAPTER FOURTEEN

(1) *THE ANTIQUITIES OF THE JEWS*; by Flavius Josephus; Book 1, Chapter VI, Published by Kregel Publications, Grand Rapids, Michigan 1960

"*The Victory Prophetic Report*" is a quarterly newsletter edited by Robert W. Faid. It will provide a biblical overview of world events and news of forthcoming books of interest. For a sample copy, complete this card and return it to us. We are eager to have you join with us as we learn what God is saying to his church in these end times.

NAME_____

ADDRESS_____

CITY, STATE, ZIP_____

TELEPHONE_____

May God Bless You!

USE THIS CARD FOR YOURSELF,

GIVE THIS CARD TO A FRIEND.

"*The Victory Prophetic Report*" is a quarterly newsletter edited by Robert W. Faid. It will provide a biblical overview of world events and news of forthcoming books of interest. For a sample copy, complete this card and return it to us. We are eager to have you join with us as we learn what God is saying to his church in these end times.

NAME_____

ADDRESS_____

CITY, STATE, ZIP_____

TELEPHONE_____

May God Bless You!